O.P.   12.50

LILIAN BAYLIS
Manager of the Old Vic from 1898 to 1937

Old Vic Saga

by

HARCOURT WILLIAMS

WITH 123 ILLUSTRATIONS
IN BLACK AND WHITE
AND A COLOUR FRONTISPIECE

WINCHESTER PUBLICATIONS LIMITED
16 Maddox Street, London, W.1

First published in mcmxlix by
Winchester Publications Limited,
16 Maddox Street, London, W.1

MADE AND PRINTED IN GREAT BRITAIN BY L. T. A. ROBINSON LTD., LONDON, S.W.9.

To
JOHN GIELGUD

The Royal Coburg Theatre
From an old engraving

CONTENTS

CONTENTS

SADLER'S WELLS THEATRE IN 1860
From an old engraving

ILLUSTRATIONS

ILLUSTRATIONS

ILLUSTRATIONS

ILLUSTRATIONS

Preface

THERE is a game one used to play round the nursery fire—a kind of gossip game. The players arrange themselves in a semi-circle. The first one whispers an item of news into the ear of his neighbour, who in his turn passes it on to the next one, and so on until it has reached the last little boy or girl. The bit of gossip is then compared with the original. The additions and embroideries that have occurred during its journey are the joke of the game. A simple form of amusement, but that is how history often comes into being. We all see facts from different angles. We add a little to make them more effective, we suppress an item because we think it better omitted.

In gathering material for this story of the Old Vic's dramatic work I have encountered considerable divergence of opinion, and although I was an eye-witness of some of the productions, that is no guarantee of infallibility on my part, and to my sins of misinterpretation must be added those of omission. Naturally, of my own years there I have been able to write with greater certainty.

The story of the opera and the ballet has been told by Professor E. J. Dent in his *A Theatre for Everybody*, and in many other publications. That I have so little to say about the opera does not mean that I am not well aware of the debt that we of the drama owe to our elder brother. Had there been no opera there would probably have been no Shakespeare at the Old Vic. It was the opera in various truncated forms that carried Emma Cons through the early days and gradually created the audience which the drama was to share. For some time the opera actually subsidized the drama as Charles Corri pointed out to me when I first went to the Old Vic as producer. Incidentally I registered a vow that I would reverse the situation and for a short time I did, as others did after me.

Proud as Lilian Baylis was of the Shakespeare company the opera was her first love, which was reasonable enough in view of her musical training. She always tried to share her affection equally between her children, however, and never would admit which was her favourite.

Many have helped me in the telling of this story. I gladly acknowledge a debt of gratitude to George Bernard Shaw, Clive Carey, Tyrone Guthrie, Sir Laurence Olivier, Irene Beeston, and Evelyn M. Williams, for permitting me to quote from their writings, to Mr T. C. Worsley and the editor of the *New Statesman and Nation* for permission to quote the passage appearing on page 211, and to many others for information and help. It is to the members of the Vic-Wells Association that I owe the tabulated lists of plays and players at the end of this book. My thanks are also due to Miss Evelyn M. Williams for reading the proofs.

And there is my wife, Jean Sterling Mackinlay, who has been untiring in reading my manuscript as it grew page by page. Her sage counsel and constructive criticism, tempered with encouragement, have been sure guides.

HARCOURT WILLIAMS

I

A Lamp is Lit

ONE summer afternoon in 1613 flames shot into the air fed by the blazing beams of British oak, and thus for some three hundred years the art of the theatre ceased to be of paramount importance on what was known then as London's Bankside, and all hope for future generations of solving the mystery that is Shakespeare went up in smoke.

The Globe theatre with its library of prompt copies, and such documentary evidence as may be found in any theatre today or yesterday, were reduced to ashes ; sacred ashes from which no phoenix was to arise until, early in the nineteenth century, a bird of little promise and melodramatic plumage raised its head on that part of the lower marsh by the south bank of the Thames which is now the junction of the New Cut and the Waterloo Road. The fledgling was christened The Royal Coburg Theatre, later to be renamed The Royal Victoria Hall.

It is at this point that women enter the field. How bad social conditions were among what were termed the lower classes is difficult to assess, but that they were a danger to the economic structure of the State became evident to thinking minds, just as it was also evident that popular opinion, principally expressed by those placed in comfort and affluence by the industrial revolution, was not interested at all.

It took a group of women—encouraged no doubt by the works of Wilkie Collins, Charles Kingsley and Dickens—to take practical steps towards alleviating those conditions. From a list of women that includes such pioneers as Elizabeth Fry, Florence Nightingale and Octavia Hill, let us take the name of Emma Cons.

It has been said that she was an enemy of the theatre. Undoubtedly she disapproved wholeheartedly of music halls as she did of gin palaces. But she was not an enemy of entertainment. She probably had no vision of what the theatre at its finest can do for humanity ; but then that is a failing not uncommon in this art-shy island.

Emma Cons hated drunkenness and the whoremongers' trade—in those days all the blame fell unfairly on those whom Victorian prudery referred to as ' fallen women '—and she hoped to win the drinkers from the brightly lit pubs and the sinners from the notorious ' promenades ' by offering them light, wholesome entertainment with coffee and buns by way of refreshment. She persuaded various philanthropists to let her have the necessary backing and although the scheme encountered several financial shoals it never actually ran aground.

By that time the Coburg Theatre had become The Royal Victoria Music Hall. Emma Cons inserted the word ' Coffee ' and thus evolved the cumbrous title of The Royal Victoria Coffee Music Hall. Later ' Coffee ' was dropped from the title though never from the bars, and then finally the word ' Music ' disappeared. The title ' The Royal Victoria Hall ' still appears on the official notepaper of the theatre ; but long since the public took the matter into their own hands and called it ' The Old Vic ', by which nickname it has become known all over the world.

The entertainment provided by Emma Cons was of a mixed nature. It was clean, wholesome, and, in its mildness, probably a little dull. The music-hall turns had to be eminently respectable. There is a legend that Emma Cons sat nightly in the prompt corner and if a ' number ' developed any impropriety she let down the old roller curtain on the delinquent's head.

For the uninitiated the ' act-drop ' in those days was made of canvas and was mounted on a heavy roller at its foot. Round the protruding ends ropes were wound and when these were pulled from the flies the unwinding ropes on the tumbler wound up the curtain in reverse action. Originally the device was probably used in theatres that had not much space in the flies. Tableau curtains (abbreviated to ' tabs ') on counterweights are mostly used today.

Lectures and penny readings, then so popular, were included in the programmes and I have heard much of those days from William Townsend, familiarly known as ' Townie ', who is the doyen of the Old Vic. His uncle was a friend of Emma Cons and so as a boy of twelve he started selling programmes. As he grew up he took on various more important jobs, such as giving a hand with a music-hall comedian's props, and painting the theatre. Now he is on the staff at Sadler's Wells. During his forty odd years he has seen many changes. The principal lighting at first was gas, with oil lamps as secondary lighting. The footlights were mantle burners, and while the audience was assembling the fireman would solemnly pass along them with a taper. Each burner lit with a resounding ' plop '. The battens over the stage were ordinary gas jets inefficiently guarded with wire netting. If the

EMMA CONS
Founder in 1880 of The Royal Victoria Hall.

THE ROYAL COBURG THEATRE
The building which was destined to become ' The Old Vic ' :
an engraving of 1819.

scene required a subdued lighting effect, the gas supply would be curtailed at the main cock. If, as sometimes happened, the gasman turned the gas too low, the scene would have to be held up while the fireman, taper in hand, again paraded to the ' plop, plop ' of the rekindled burners.

Much of Townie's painting activities were shared with Bob Robinson. ' Old Bob ', as we came to know him in our day, was a period piece. He worked at the Old Vic from the earliest days, first as stage carpenter and, in his old age, as stage doorkeeper. He belonged to the Victorian ' working classes ' that *Punch* used to patronize in the 'eighties and which the socialism (with a dash of William Morris in it) of Emma Cons had striven to uplift. It was for Bob and his kind that the Old Vic had been invented. I believe that it has been one of the unrealized difficulties of that memorable institution that his type now scarcely can be said to exist. However that was the notion in those days of a new democracy, which Lilian Baylis shared. ' We're not particular about Miss and Mister down here,' she would say.

Bob enjoyed displaying his homely South London idiosyncrasies, and although he was never discourteous, he treated one and all as

THE OLD VIC
In 1931, the established ' home of Shakespeare ' in London,
under the management of Lilian Baylis.

equals. He reminded me of Edward Carpenter's friend George. When
I met George late in life, I found him just a shade too boisterous in his
insistence on democratic comradeship. But Old Bob was not a little
proud of his associations with the great ones who had come to the theatre
to help the good cause in the past. When my wife used to sing at the
Old Vic he would regale her with some familiar anecdote about
Antoinette Sterling. With a twinkling eye he would draw her into the
stage doorkeeper's office—' The mother said to me, Bob, she says . . . '
And perhaps he would tell again how, when Madame Sterling first
came to sing there and was told that the audience smoked, she had
urged that she could not sing in such an atmosphere ; shag was
pretty strong in those days.

' But we daren't stop them,' explained the management, ' they are
far too rough a crowd to put up with interference.' Antoinette Sterling
walked on to the stage and, with her rare smile, said : ' I want to sing
to you, but if I do, all this smoke will hurt my voice. Now if you like
your pipes better than my singing, why, you just go on smoking.' And
every pipe was knocked out.

I was once introduced to a family in Camberwell. The father, who was a clockmaker, invited me to have a cup of tea with them at their evening meal. When the friend who had brought me there told them that I was married to the daughter of Antoinette Sterling, they all rose from their seats. 'We always stand when that name is mentioned,' explained the old man.

It is easy enough to smile at those philanthropic God-fearing women in these very different days, but it was precisely the love and reverence that they inspired that made the coffee-and-buns experiment a success. Emma Cons may not have been aware of it, but the bait that she was dangling to lure men and women from vice was the very essence of the theatre—what Harley Granville-Barker called the miracle of human communion, and for which he asserted he would gladly sit through a whole evening of indifferent acting for five minutes of the real thing.

Managers came and went under Miss Cons. No doubt navigating an experimental ship of this kind in a sea full of financial rocks required greater ability than the salary could command. The name of one manager who worked there longer than most, which must mean that he was a success, has become a landmark in the history of the Theatre ; and although no Shakespeare was done at the Old Vic in his time, it was there that the Elizabethan method of presenting the plays was used long before it became fashionable in the West End.

This reformer in embryo was, of course, William Poel. I fancy he must have been at the Old Vic round about 1886 for two years. He was born on July 22, 1852, so he was still a young man and much of his work lay before him ; but in February 1881 he had played Hamlet in a matinee performance at the St George's Hall in which the text of the First Quarto edition was used. This was the first revival of the draped stage in this country or elsewhere. Poel had been an actor for four years or so. A conservative Press did not seem to think that he was good in the title role, but the opinion was probably prejudiced. His 'Ofelia' was Maud Holt, the future Lady Tree. I have not the smallest doubt that Poel's ideals finally had a lasting influence on the Old Vic's approach to Shakespeare. Bernard Shaw writing half a century ago said, ' What a gigantic reform Mr Poel will make if his Elizabethan Stage should lead to such a novelty as a theatre to which people go to see the play instead of the cast.' A reform for which most of us are still waiting !

And then in 1895 occurred an event without apparent purpose—an accident. Miss Cons had a niece who lived and worked in South Africa teaching music and dancing. She was not making the best headway after an illness and her aunt invited her to visit England for a holiday. The holiday ended in the longest working day of her life,

THE ROYAL VICTORIA HALL

In 1922, Morley College (on the right) still occupied the back of the building, and the nickname the 'Old Vic' (displayed beneath the clock on the left) had not yet displaced the title given to the theatre by Emma Cons.

for she took on the management of the Old Vic under Emma Cons. Her name was Lilian Baylis. Was it an accident? Or a hand on fortune's wheel?

The story of how Lilian Baylis came to the Old Vic to help her aunt has been told many times. She obviously shared the same point of view and the same religious enthusiasms. Much has been said of the parading of her faith, and from my own knowledge I fancy this side of her has been much overstated. She expressed her religion through the conventional phraseology of the Church, but her fundamental faith went a good deal deeper than that. Nor, in the four years I worked with her, did she once question my faith or indulge in any of the legendary 'kneelings in prayer' so often quoted.

When I was on the point of joining the Old Vic Edith Craig said to me, 'Wait until L. B. asks you to pray with her.' But she never did. The nearest approach to any such occurrence was one day when, more than usually pressed for funds, she exclaimed to me, 'I must find some money. I keep praying for money, but the Almighty only sends me penny collections.'

ROYAL VISIT

Their Majesties King George V and Queen Mary, then Prince and Princess of Wales, at The Royal Victoria Hall, March 3, 1910. Lilian Baylis can be seen in the box on the left of the second tier, and Emma Cons on the right of the first tier of boxes.

I knew that she occasionally went into retreat at some religious establishment in the country—a period of rest for all of us on the executive side !—and yet I had an indefinable feeling that I did not like that office of hers being empty.

I scarcely ever met Father Andrew, and the only other parson I remember was the kind vicar of St John's in the Waterloo Road, familiarly known to us as Father Hutch (the Rev. Canon C. W. Hutchinson). So at that period at least no one can say we were Church-ridden.

Emma Cons died in 1912. Her portrait, which used to hang in the vestibule at the Old Vic, shows a strong, simple face under a Victorian bonnet such as Madge Kendal used to delight in. She wears a jacket of the period with sleeves built up at the shoulders. It is not the face of a genius, but one can read in it a steadfastness of purpose and the calm of goodwill. Nearby hung a portrait of King George V. 'Not quite so large as Aunt Emma's,' Lilian Baylis once explained to Queen Mary, ' because your dear husband has not done so much for the Old Vic.'

Recitals of operas already had an important place in the programmes and it was only the licensing laws that made it impossible to give them in their proper form with a full stage production. Charles Corri had arrived on the scene by this time and very great credit is due to his industry and ingenuity in arranging the scores for small orchestras and overcoming what many would have found insuperable difficulties. Later Lilian Baylis obtained a dramatic licence so that the operas could be given in full, and when Shakespeare crossed the threshold, Mr Corri became responsible for the incidental music in the plays as well as the opera. He continued to hold a position that must have been not only strenuous but one which also required unlimited tact, until he relinquished the baton to the rising generation of conductors at Sadler's Wells.

The other important attraction was the showing of early essays in films. Lilian Baylis was one of the first to foster this new-born babe of science and the child did very well indeed until other theatres with better equipment began to show pictures of a wider range than she approved of.

It was then that this astute manager began to look around for some other attraction to fill the bill. How exactly she came to Shakespeare must remain an unsolved mystery. It is on record that she once said, ' I had lost so much money that in despair I turned to Shakespeare.' I don't think she was ever in any sense a student of the plays. Granville-Barker made a guess that she knew nothing of them, but that ' she had a way '. She certainly had.

There seems to have been a single performance of *The Merchant of Venice* even earlier than Rosina Filippi's brief season. It was arranged

MATHESON LANG
Producer at the theatre with his wife, Hutin Britton, in 1914.

by Charles Fry, a celebrated reciter. I have a vague suspicion that Hermione Gingold played Jessica on this occasion to the Shylock of Michael Sherbrooke, which leads me to believe that one day she will return to play Lady Macbeth when she is weary of playing the 'cello !

The celebrated Stratford-on-Avon producer, W. Bridges-Adams, and a friend from Oxford, George Owen, brought forward a scheme for doing Shakespeare plays, but the scheme came to nothing because cautious Miss Baylis was taking no risks and demanded a guarantee which the young men could not pay. The boys had been working in Laurence Irving's company. He was the younger son of Henry Irving, and when he went down with the *Empress of Ireland*, the theatre lost a very remarkable actor and the Old Vic possibly his brilliant influence.

Rosina Filippi is the next personality to enter. She was a player of great ability and high standing as a character actress. She was a woman who put up with no nonsense, but her forthright character was tempered with great humour. I well remember her rich chuckle when she complained to me of ' this modern lighting. I want light on my face, not on my stomach ! '

She obtained permission to have the theatre for one night a week and the first production was, I believe, *Romeo and Juliet*. Later she put on *The School for Scandal*, which seems to have startled the Governors of the Old Vic, but when Bernard Shaw's *Candida* was to be added to the repertoire they were positively shocked. A storm seems to have blown up and echoes of it were heard in the Press. I have no doubt that Miss Filippi expressed her point of view in no uncertain terms, and the arrangement came to an end.

As far as I can discover *Candida* was not actually produced and it would seem that it was my productions of *Androcles and the Lion* and *The Dark Lady of the Sonnets* in 1930 which first introduced Bernard Shaw's plays to the Old Vic.

The audiences in the early days were sometimes very meagre, especially for the educational lectures. So on those occasions a set of curtains, hung underneath the circle, were drawn round to shut out the empty cavern of the pit. But these lectures were truly bread cast upon the waters. One night two boys made their way behind the scenes and asked Emma Cons if they could learn more than they were able to pick up at the penny lectures. She at once arranged for an evening class to be held in one of the disused dressing-rooms. From this small beginning the attendances rapidly increased, and students, their books and their teachers overflowed all over the theatre to the embarrassment of the opera singers and the other theatre workers. In 1889 the back of the theatre was walled off, and a college took definite shape. It was christened Morley College in memory of Samuel Morley, whose beneficence had been one of the principal financial standbys in the early days of the Emma Cons enterprise.

In 1923 the college moved to its present site, since badly damaged by enemy action, and the Old Vic was able to rebuild its dressing-rooms and create convenient offices.

Early in 1948 an elderly man named J. C. Sparkhall visited Morley College in its present position in the Westminster Bridge Road. He seemed so greatly interested in its activities that he was asked the reason. ' I was one of the boys who started it,' he replied.

Before this, however, about the spring of 1914, a great appeal was launched for financial aid, chiefly to promote the opera side of the entertainment. Shakespeare—except for the Filippi flutter—was still non-existent. Some £800 had been collected when the first World War shattered all further hopes. It was about this time that Matheson Lang consented to put on some Shakespeare plays with his wife Hutin Britton, who later became a Governor of the Old Vic. One of the plays chosen was *The Merchant of Venice*. I played Gratiano when Lang gave it in 1915 at the St James's. I remember it as a colourful production, a trifle overloaded with scenery as the fashion then called for. The little scene of Shylock's first bargaining with Antonio, for example, was moved into an inset of Shylock's house. But Lang was a very good actor and his Shylock well worth seeing. The Old Vic audience must have gaped indeed at the gorgeous West End scenery and dresses—very different from the stock wings which they knew by heart. The other plays presented by Matheson Lang were *The Taming of the Shrew* and *Hamlet*. These performances must have driven a good sound wedge into the minds of the audiences and opened the way for new ideas on what entertainment might mean. They also were a good education for Miss Baylis. Many agreed with Granville-Barker that she knew nothing about Shakespeare at that time, but although she may never have watched a single performance right through, or even read a play from beginning to end, she certainly acquired a very businesslike knowledge of his practicabilities as a playwright, and not a little rough commonsense insight into some of the characters.

In due course the Matheson Langs had to leave to fulfil other engagements, and according to the published Annual Report of 1914-15 various people gave a hand in the Shakespeare work and production, notably Fisher White, Ben Webster, Lady Benson (then Mrs F. R. Benson), Mrs Edward Compton (Miss Fay Compton's mother), and Miss Estelle Stead who not only acted for the Old Vic but produced and raised funds. Miss Stead was the daughter of the famous editor of the *Review of Reviews* and it was she who thought of asking Ben Greet (later Sir Philip Ben Greet) to come and work there.

Later in the Report indebtedness is recorded to Mrs Wordsworth for arranging the dances in *The Tempest* and *A Midsummer Night's Dream*. Mrs Wordsworth was a conspicuous figure in my generation. Very few children round and about London and even in the provinces had not attended Mrs Wordsworth's dancing classes. By a strange coincidence one of these children was Ninette de Valois who was to work for the Old Vic and make brilliant history at Sadler's Wells. Mrs Wordsworth had somehow lost an eye and when she looked at her watch, a very small

'THE MERCHANT OF VENICE'
The first recorded production of the play at the Royal Victoria Hall (as the Old Vic then was) was that directed, in 1914, by Matheson Lang and his wife, Hutin Britton.

one, towards the end of a class she would hold it right up to the good eye. My own memory is of rather a terrifying person, though I was not actually afraid of her. It was almost as shattering to be called out to give a solo exhibition because one was good, as to be singled out from the back rows, where one hoped to be hidden, and reprimanded for not swinging the Indian clubs with enough vigour. A rather sweet-faced lady, who was slightly lame and dressed in bonnet and mantle like an early du Maurier drawing, accompanied us on the worn-out upright piano. Mrs Wordsworth always screamed her commands, probably to get them heard above the din of the piano and the many rustling feet. I somehow connected her with Alice's Red Queen.

SIR PHILIP BEN GREET
Producer at the theatre during the war years 1914-18.

28

II

The Game Begins

BEN GREET had been touring his own companies both in Britain and the States for many years and had handled all the better known Shakespeare plays. He brought with him to the Old Vic many of his own people who knew the plays well. Consequently, as he never wanted to alter anything in the way of stage business or reading of parts, it was possible to put on a number of plays in fairly quick succession.

Soon after Ben Greet started work an event of great consequence to the Old Vic occurred. He wrote the following letter to a young actress whom he had previously had in his company.

'There's a strange woman running a theatre in the Waterloo Road . . . you will find her exciting because you are as mad as she is. I'm doing some shows for her with Estelle Stead, so come and join us . . . You'll like Lilian Baylis, she's got ideals . . .'

The letter was addressed to Dame Sybil Thorndike.

It was in the autumn of 1914 that she entered that surprising theatre and stayed there for four years playing an equally surprising round of parts, including a few of the male sex. At first the company did three plays a week, and two nights were devoted to performances at Bethnal Green in a converted swimming bath and at the Northern Polytechnic, Holloway.

I ran across Sir Philip on one or two occasions before I came to know him as a friend. When I was very young he wrote to me to ask if I would care to take over his company while he visited America. To my suggestion that I would like to look at the ' books ', he replied, ' Books ! I don't keep any books. Money goes into my pocket and I pay it out again.' I did not then know that his nature was as simple and honest as that statement. Later I met him as a producer when he was putting on *The Winter's Tale* for a Sunday society called The Fellowship

Players.   Dame Lilian Braithwaite was the Hermione, Angela Baddeley,
Perdita, and I was the Leontes.   Everything was done as it had always
been done in the Ben Greet companies.   Indeed, he had some of his
old players filling the minor roles.   With great difficulty I persuaded
him to let me put back most of the text which had been cut in accordance
with mid-Victorian ideas of purity.   He thought the lines were quite
unnecessary and would be no help to my performance.   Perhaps he was
right.   Certainly The Fellowship Players never survived that night !

But B.G. was very amiable and easy to work for, as he sat comfortably
in the stalls and dived into his bag of sweets while giving occasional
directions.   In spite of his rather careless performances he knew his
Shakespeare inside out.   He told me once he found a Maria wearing a
string of amber beads.   Before making his entrance as Malvolio he
whispered ' Take those beads off, my dear.'

' Why should I ? ' answered Maria.   ' I like them and they suit the
dress.'

' Take 'em off, my dear.'   And as his cue came for his entrance to

ROBERT ATKINS
An early appearance as Sir Toby Belch.
He first acted at the Old Vic in 1915.

FLORENCE SAUNDERS
A much-loved Old Vic actress from 1916
to 1921, and the season of 1923-4.

ESTELLE STEAD
As Rosalind in *As You Like It*, 1915. She played at the theatre throughout the first World War.

WILLIAM STACK
In *The Taming of the Shrew*, 1914-15. He was a member of Ben Greet's company until 1916.

Olivia, he hissed over his shoulder, 'Yellow stockings, a colour she abhors !'

The list of players with established reputations who flocked to the Old Vic standard during the first war years (1914-15) is impressive. Thirteen plays of Shakespeare were given, as well as *She Stoops to Conquer* and *The School for Scandal*.

Children from schools were beginning to attend, many of them from the L.C.C. schools. The opera seems to have been doing very well. 'At several performances the gratifying notice (from a managerial standpoint) of " Standing room only " has been seen outside the Hall [sic] by 8 o'clock' says the Annual Report. But it adds, 'We must point out that the very large audiences do not mean a profit owing to the low prices charged.' And one senses the guiding hand of Lilian Baylis.

During the Ben Greet régime, which lasted until the beginning of 1918, the veteran actor Fisher White came to do some producing and also to play Macbeth.

Two little excursions at this time have to be recorded—the first tentative steps across the puddles of the New Cut into the brave wide world. The first was to Stratford-on-Avon, with *Macbeth*, *The Winter's Tale*, *As You Like It* and *The Two Gentlemen of Verona*. This was of course for the Birthday Celebrations. Owing to an overlapping in management two Lady Macbeths had been engaged, Nancy Price by Archibald Flower and Sybil Thorndike by Lilian Baylis. The difficulty, however, was solved by their playing the part on alternate nights. The second outing was to the Theatre Royal, Portsmouth. The company seems to have done well in a six weeks' season there. Afterwards the company ran a commonwealth, at what Dame Sybil describes as 'that funny old theatre at Portsmouth', playing ' *Oliver Twist* twice nightly for three weeks'. It was of course the high-spirited Thorndike enthusiasm that brought this about and also their return to the Old Vic for a short spell with Russell Thorndike as Sherlock Holmes !

Lilian Baylis had a fertile brain for inventing ways of advertising the Old Vic without a great outlay of cash. It was a long time, however, before she would consent to invite critics or in any way to woo the Press or value the publicity that it could give her. I am reminded of an aristocratic old lady who arranged a public performance for me at Exmouth when I was in my twenties. When I arrived with my company she greeted me with the news that the house was sold out, and that a newspaper man from Exeter had asked for details about us and for a seat. ' I sent him away with a flea in his ear ! ' she exclaimed exultantly.

Tom Kealey, who had been interested in Sybil Thorndike, offered to do some publicity work for the Old Vic for nothing ; but at first Lilian would not accept. She thought it would involve her in advertising in the daily papers, and she was of the opinion that if the newspapers were really fond of opera and Shakespeare they should put the advertisements in free of charge. However at last she agreed. Fortunately she was never too obstinate to change her mind, as Russell Thorndike said. Tom Kealey at first found it difficult to get the Press to come until he persuaded George Morrison of the *Morning Post* to do so. After the first visit he came every week and glowing notices began to appear. Then the others followed, Walkley, Archer and St John Ervine among them. Up went the business and packed houses began to occur.

Before this the chief means of spreading the good tidings was by the Green Leaflet. This flimsy ' throw-away ' became an integral part of the Old Vic. When it was instituted I cannot say. Some say it began as a yellow leaflet, others that it was ever green. It was some ten inches by five and a half inches in size, and gave in tabulated form the dates of the forthcoming operas, plays, and any special lectures and recitals. The ballets, of course, came later. Then there were the prices of the seats—in the early days ranging from a twopenny gallery to a two-shilling stall—and the dates of the rare occasions when advertisements might be found in the daily papers. Indeed a great deal of information was crowded into this small leaflet. It was printed on both sides on rather thin green paper and was headed THE OLD VIC : THE HOME OF SHAKESPEARE AND OPERA IN ENGLISH, with acknowledgements to the founder, Emma Cons, and the lessee and manager, Lilian Baylis, with her appropriate titles as they occurred. Not a single letter left the building without one of these leaflets tucked into the envelope. Batches of them lay by the box-office window, and a bundle on Lilian Baylis's desk. In the days when little or nothing could be spent on advertising, the leaflet was an excellent means of publicity. Its one drawback was that it tied the management to a definite programme extending over many weeks. If a play did exceptionally well there was no possibility of taking advantage of the success, or, on the other hand, of curtailing a failure. It was not until the arrival of Tyrone Guthrie that this survival of the parochial period met its match. In ideal conditions a repertory company should be prepared to stick to its guns, but, truth to tell, we could not afford to lose money.

Perhaps it will give some idea of the financial position when I say that in Robert Atkins's day the average cost of the scenery and costumes for each production was under £15, and in my day about £20.

There were other shreds and patches left over from the Emma Cons régime. Between the acts lantern slides advertising future plans would be thrown on the safety curtain. They were crude in design and entailed the lowering of the house lights just when the audience wanted to look at their programmes. It had a depressing effect and took an electrician's only assistant away just when he was wanted to change the stage lighting for the next act.

There were two other ingenious schemes for building up the audiences. One was the Old Vic Magazine which formed a liaison between the management, the players and the public. It was first issued in October 1919. I do not know who originally undertook the editorial responsibility but it was later in the experienced hands of Irene Beeston.

Then there were the Circle and the Association—social groups or clubs among the audience. The Circle embraced the gallery and the pit ; the Association the more expensive seats. These seem to have been founded in 1923. When Sadler's Wells was opened a society was started there, chiefly to induce the inhabitants of Islington to patronize the stalls ; but later the various interests were amalgamated in the present Vic-Wells Association.

Before the departure of Sir Philip Ben Greet the Old Vic celebration of Shakespeare's birthday had come into being. It became an established event in the calendar of every season as long as Miss Baylis was alive. The box office knew that on the first and last nights of the season, and on the ' Birthday ' night, the house would be sold out. The Birthday night programme consisted of snippets and scenes. Players who had worked for the Old Vic poured over Waterloo Bridge from all parts of London. Some, clad in their stage costumes, hurried in taxis from West End theatres. The job of the producer and stage manager in fitting all these odd scenes together and arranging times to suit those who had to be there and away with only seconds to spare was a hair-raising occupation. I have before me a programme of one of these nights. It is not dated but I think it was for 1917.

It starts with the overture to *The Merry Wives of Windsor* to the accompaniment of fifteen pictures of Stratford-on-Avon. (Or should it be pictures accompanied by the overture ?) A song follows, and a scene from *As You Like It* with Sybil Thorndike as Rosalind and her brother as Touchstone. Then Miss Nellie Chaplin gives a selection of Shakespearean dances. Lilian Braithwaite is down for Portia in *Julius Caesar*, and her daughter Joyce Carey as Lucius. While the next scene is being set two more songs from Shakespeare hold the fort, sung by Constance Willis who, if she was not already so, was to become a leading light in the opera company. An excerpt from *King John* follows, with Mrs Matheson Lang as Constance, and, surprisingly, Florence Saunders as the old Queen Elinor. Florence Saunders has become a kind of legend to Old Vic-ites. She had a very lovable nature and she was affectionately known to all as ' Dickie '. Maybe the fact that she, a young and beautiful girl, had volunteered to ' go on ' as cantankerous old Elinor was a reflection of her good nature. One whose opinion I value says she was the most beautiful woman she had ever seen— ' standing against a grape-coloured curtain on an empty stage with her dark hair flowing to her knees '.

Dickie married John Laurie, who was to become so intimately connected with the theatre. Alas, she was one of those whom the gods loved. Another in the cast for whom ' the abhorréd shears slit the thin spun life too soon ' was Eric Ross. Sybil Thorndike, Ernest Milton and many others thought Ross had a brilliant future. ' It was the larger sweep of a part that Lilian usually perceived,' writes Sybil, ' the thing that she translated immediately into terms of the world she knew, but with these two she noticed the smallest, most homely details.'

But the Birthday programme is not yet over. (Oh yes, it was always a very long evening's entertainment.) Gertrude Elliott (Lady Forbes-

REHEARSAL

Ben Greet rehearsing Sybil Thorndike as the Queen and Russell Thorndike as Hamlet in the ' Closet ' scene from the play—a special performance in aid of the Sadler's Wells Fund in 1926.

Robertson) does the balcony scene with Ben Webster as Romeo. (Dear Ben Webster, descendant of such an honourable line of players ; so courteous and debonair to the last. We who knew you salute your passing.) The indefatigable Russell Thorndike bobs up again as Launce with Crab, the dog, in an interlude from *The Two Gentlemen of Verona*, and finally the curtain rings up on scenes from *The Merchant of Venice*. The ' set piece ' at the Crystal Palace on Brock's benefit night

WILLIAM POEL

'A lasting influence on the Old Vic's approach to Shakespeare'. From the painting by Professor Henry Tonks of Poel as Father Keegan in the Shaw play, John Bull's Other Island.

could not have aroused more enthusiasm, more exclamations of delight, more cries of ' ΟΥΟΥ ! '

Matheson Lang is the Shylock, Henry Vibart the Antonio, Jean Sterling Mackinlay the Nerissa, Tom Heslewood the Doge, and, wonder of wonders, Ellen Terry herself as Portia. Even the ' crowd ' is exciting. We find the names of Ellen Terry's grandchildren, Teddy and Nellie, her daughter Edith, Christopher St John, Clare Atwood, Leah Bateman, great-granddaughter of Irving's Colonel Bateman, and Beatrice Wilson, of whom there is more to be said.

So ends the Birthday programme with all the players and the audience singing 'God Save the King' . . . with unexpected words. The first verse was as usual, the second was called the 'American Verse' and the last was applicable to the war which was still raging. Yes, a long exhausting evening indeed. I sometimes felt that the birthday boy was perhaps a little overlooked in the general excitement, but it undoubtedly gave the supporters of the Old Vic very real happiness to welcome again their old favourites, many of whom had, since crossing the Thames, set that ancient stream on fire.

Another 'institution' that had become an annual event was the performance of *Everyman* during the last week of Lent. William Poel had discovered the manuscript of this medieval morality play, and since he had produced it in London at the beginning of this century it had become world-famous. I remember being deeply moved by it, but I did not care for a woman playing the part of Everyman, though it was finely done by Wynne Matheson. The grim figure of Death beating on his drum thrilled me, but Sybil Thorndike, who was cast for Everyman at the Old Vic, tells how an audience of monks in Santa Barbara laughed at the character, and she advances the theory that to the medieval audience he was accepted as a comic one. During the constant revivals many men played Everyman—Swinley, Milton, Holloway and others— and as the play is very short a speaker of note used to be invited to address the audience as a kind of prologue. Among the names of these speakers I find Maude Royden, Sir Johnston Forbes-Robertson, Henry Ainley, Sheila Kaye-Smith, Cicely Hamilton, Viscountess Rhondda, Clemence Dane and G. K. Chesterton.

It is I think of some significance that on April 24, 1917, William Poel is advertised on the back of the Old Vic programme to lecture on 'Stage Costumes in Shakespeare's Day'. Although he had left the Old Vic some years before and had had no opportunity of stage direction, yet his theories were to find expression in the future work of the theatre and to be of no little assistance. It was Poel who made the first attack on the over-upholstered, pseudo-archaeologically correct way of staging Shakespeare, which had led to the drastic cutting of the plays and the general slowing up of the tempo to fit it all into the elaborate scenery. Just before the 1914 war Granville-Barker had led us a step farther by showing us magnificent performances of *Twelfth Night* and *The Winter's Tale*. And there is no doubt that the brilliant work which was to be done by Robert Atkins when he arrived at the Old Vic was based on Poel's conception of the Elizabethan theatre.

The next producer was G. R. Foss. His reign was a short one from 1918 to the summer of 1919, but he left behind him a reputation for a scholarly understanding of Shakespeare. He was well known for his work with the O.U.D.S. and his productions won high praise. At the Old Vic he probably found things vastly different from those at Oxford. The scenery was worse than negligible, the costumes were such as one expected from cheap hiring, and, of course, there was no money to spend.

Indeed, as one reads through the official Annual Reports of the Old Vic from the very beginning, the articles dealing with the accounts reveal an unending struggle to make both ends meet. Had it not been for various grants and appeals the ends, far from meeting, would never have had a sight of each other. One wonders at first how the Governors had the courage or the spirit to discuss any other problem or agree to any constructive plan, until one remembers that an indomitable woman drove them forward and kindled their enthusiasm with the fire of her own faith. Those who in the old days accused Lilian Baylis of parsimony might have changed their minds had they thought a little about that quarter of a century of struggle with pounds, shillings and pence.

Although great praise must be accorded Ben Greet for his work through the difficult war years of 1914-18, it was probably of the hackneyed variety (indeed it could not have been anything else in the circumstances), relieved by the young brilliance of the Thorndikes and others. G. R. Foss was, I suspect, the first to give the work some definite shape and lead it towards a much higher standard. By that time Lilian Baylis and Shakespeare were becoming better acquainted, and she was wise enough to make no bones about any deficiency of her own, but to set about removing it. She did in the end acquire a very homely understanding of the plays and one that in some respects was no farther from the author's intentions than that of certain erudite professors. At that time, however, she found Foss's ideas on casting strange. I expect Ben Greet, *faute de mieux*, had fitted round pegs into round holes and anyone attempting to force one into a square hole puzzled her. Sybil Thorndike tells us that Foss had a great sense of the theatre and often introduced challenging new readings. She adds that he made skilful use of personalities, strange and perhaps unwieldy in the ordinary sense, using for the first time completely unlikely people in well known parts. ' He's potty,' was Miss Baylis's comment. ' Fancy casting So-and-so for that part ! He'll cop it in the Press.' But he didn't and, as always, she stuck loyally by the new ways.

I was reprehensibly slow in becoming aware of the Old Vic. It was not until the spring of 1919 that I paid my first visit. The play was Foss's production of *Love's Labour's Lost* and I was taken by a young master of the Perse School, Cambridge, Caldwell Cook by name. He was a remarkable teacher and should have gone farther than he did. He published an intriguing book on education called *The Playway*, in which

THE OLD VIC COMPANY AT THE STRATFORD-ON-AVON FESTIVAL, 1916
Second row, centre : Lilian Baylis ; on her right, Ben Greet, Claire Pauncefort and Robert Atkins ; on her left, Sybil Thorndike and Florence Saunders. Behind Lilian Baylis stands Jerrold Robertshaw, with Ion Swinley on his left. Russell Thorndike holds the dog to the left of the back row.

there are chapters on acting Shakespeare in the classroom, playmaking, miming and ballads. I think he called his acting class the Mummery and the boys were invited to array themselves out of a trunk full of an odd assortment of costumes, and act to their hearts' content.

Once Mr Badley, the famous founder of Bedales, expressed a wish to visit this class. By some unlucky accident Caldwell Cook overslept himself, but on arriving breathless in the classroom he found the boys carrying out the usual curriculum, all unconscious of the austere and silent stranger sitting in their master's chair. Badley declared that nothing could have given him a better example of the success of Caldwell Cook's methods.

But to return to *Love's Labour's Lost*. My keenest recollections of that evening are a spirited performance of Biron by a young Ernest Milton, the loveliness of Florence Saunders, and the good fun of the worthies in the last act.

G. R. Foss was the brother of a first-rate actor who used the name of Charles Fulton. Fulton had a magnificent, deep voice which he could use very wittily in comedy as well as in more serious matter. But then all the family had good voices. There was a brother who was once Mayor of Croydon, and as a boy I used to hear him coming out of his house a quarter of a mile away !

III

Gaslight Nights

IN the autumn of 1919 Russell Thorndike returned to the Old Vic as co-producer with Charles Warburton, and the two of them shared the leading parts. Sometimes they alternated them, which is an interesting thing to do though trying for the supporting company. The central character of a Shakespearean play inevitably sets the tone for the whole play, and the characters concerned with the hero have to adjust their readings accordingly and with probably very few rehearsals. I found this out when I did the same thing in my time, and cast Robert Harris and Robert Speaight for Hamlet in the same production.

An interesting newcomer this season was Wilfrid Walter. Lilian Baylis told him at the audition that he was very stiff but supposed that was because he had been standing at attention for four years. He acted for nothing for six weeks and then it was discovered that he could paint, so he was given four pounds a week and put on to resuscitate the scenery which badly needed restoration. Having destroyed things for the previous four years—there was time allowed for that too, as well as for standing at attention—Walter found this an enormous relief to his spirit, but when he learned that he was also expected to act for his small fee he struck, and in the end two pounds was added to his pay-packet. His scenery made a stir in the Press, and he rose to playing leading parts and returned more than once in later years.

It was in this season that the Battle of the Grooves was fought, which is so entertainingly described in the Thorndikes' book about Lilian Baylis. The grooves were old-fashioned devices for holding up the wings and the back scene. Something of the kind is still in use at the *Comédie Française*. Lilian Baylis did not want to get rid of the grooves because of the expense involved ; and, of course, iron braces and counterweights would have to be bought to replace them. However, the boys won a half-consent out of her and at six o'clock next morning the men began the work of destruction which—according to the saga of the Thorndikes—was

RUSSELL THORNDIKE
Co-producer, with Charles Warburton, at the Old Vic, 1919-20.

41

completed exactly as the surprised and indignant Lilian Baylis arrived on the scene four hours later.

A sequence of the historical plays was given in this year, for the first time since Benson had achieved it at Stratford-on-Avon in 1901. Though incomplete, as Benson's was, the sequence ran from *Richard II* to *Henry V*; but the high peak of the season was *Coriolanus*. Warburton seems to have done well in the title role and Miss Geneviève Ward came across the river to appear as Volumnia. Between them they packed the theatre at every performance. Remembering how slow the public is to express interest in a Shakespeare play with which it is not quite familiar, this was indeed an achievement. I did not see this production but I was in the cast on several occasions when Miss Ward came into the provinces to act Volumnia in the Benson company round about 1900. And she *did* act it ! Her vitality was dynamic. The sweep of her entrance to greet her victorious son on his return from the Volscian war was ecstatic and triumphant. As she first entered telling the great news her eyes flashed excitement, and her gaiety as she told of the letters that had come was infectious. And who that heard it can forget the scornful retort to Virgilia's weak, ' The gods grant them true ! ' or the curl of her lip on the final syllables : ' True ? *Pow wow* ! ' On the reverse of the medal there was her entrance after the banishment of Coriolanus when Rome was in danger. How she strode on to the stage to pour the vials of her wrath on the two Tribunes, brilliantly played by young Oscar Asché and Arthur Grenville ! She was a small woman but she had a way of holding her head and whole body so as to dominate the scene. She could well exclaim : ' . . . lament as I do, in anger, Juno-like ', as with blazing eyes she swept from the stage. The celebrated scene in Coriolanus's tent when Volumnia, hand in hand with his wife and child, comes to plead to him to spare Rome was not quite so successful. One was conscious of her technique, and the deep maternal sympathy was lacking.

Her technique was always exemplary as I learned at my first meeting with her. For the layman I must explain that it is an old precept that the actor should kneel on the knee nearest the audience. It is not always essential but the reason is that the actor then has his face thrown slightly towards the auditorium which allows the spectator to see his expression and hear better what he has to say. One morning, about 1900, Miss Ward travelled to the provinces to play Volumnia for the first time in the Benson company which was then at the zenith of its fame. Having seen her act several roles at the Lyceum with Irving I regarded her with special awe. At the first meeting of Coriolanus with his mother he kneels to her, and, as Benson flung himself on his knee,

WILFRID WALTER

The actor at work on the scenery in his early days at the Old Vic. He
rose to playing leading parts—and also created a stir with his settings.

Miss Ward, to my surprise and consternation, instead of speaking the
text, ' Nay, my good soldier, up ', said ' Other knee, sonnie.' It was
a staggering moment for us youngsters to witness our chief, whose wont
it was to admonish us, himself admonished ! But Benson with a smile
changed to the other knee and the scene continued.

When Miss Ward played Volumnia with Benson she was on the way
to seventy ; when she played at the Old Vic she was eighty-three.
From all I hear and from what I knew of her the vigour of her performance
was undiminished.

Sybil Thorndike and Lewis Casson gave some matinees of *The
Trojan Women* during this season. The décor was by Bruce Winston and
the venture proved so successful that they migrated to the Holborn
Empire ; there, and in other theatres, they became responsible for
memorable productions of which I imagine *St Joan* was the greatest.

43

By this time the opera had grown out of its beginnings of costume recitals and *tableaux vivants*. It was firmly established and an important factor in the financial resources of the theatre. Though still largely supported by amateur and part-time workers, by Charles Corri and the enthusiasm of the leading singers, the standard was slowly but surely rising. Wherever one digs into the past of the Old Vic one finds people wrestling with difficulties that would seem insurmountable to many. Clive Carey when he joined the opera company in 1919 speaks of rudimentary scenery and dresses.

'We were chiefly dependent on what fell from the crumbs of the Shakespeare company which we felt for many years was Miss Baylis's favourite child. Conditions were terribly difficult. It was often impossible to get sufficient rehearsals . . . the stage was so frequently needed by the Shakespeare company, and it was very disheartening to arrive for a performance and find that the most important piece of scenery had been painted a different colour for use in a play.'

There was always supposed to be a feud between the opera and the Shakespeare company but I don't think it was very serious. We also suffered from having favourite properties and convenient stage seats taken away from us for essential use in opera, and, of course, the doubling of boots and shoes in the wardrobe was a constant agony, especially as Orlando, the famous wardrobe master, had a method of smiling down the strongest representations. Owing to the working schedule of a theatre alternating opera and drama we were inevitably forced to live a Box and Cox existence and so, socially, we never met except at the annual garden party at her Stockwell home when Lilian Baylis flung us into each other's arms . . . two strange children told to play together at a party would give a lifelike picture of the result.

Up to the date of the alterations to the back of the theatre when Morley College departed to the Westminster Bridge Road the discomfort behind the scenes beggars description. I know because I actually witnessed it. At one time my wife (Jean Sterling Mackinlay) gave annual recitals at the Old Vic and I assisted. I forget when the first one took place but it was certainly before 1923. She dressed in a narrow slip of a room on the stage which must have been used by Sybil Thorndike and others. It was so small that Jean could hardly turn round in it and her dresser was put to it to know where to hang her dresses. Besides this there was Miss Baylis's office which I believe she vacated in the evening for opera leads and thus formed her habit of camping in the box during performances, a habit that was never to be broken. Later when Sadler's Wells was reopened she had a small office at the back of the

GENEVIÈVE WARD AS VOLUMNIA
She came to the Old Vic to give her famous interpretation of the part in *Coriolanus* during the 1919-20 season.

circle (there are no boxes there) with a peephole that gave a distant view of the stage. But she did not like it. She always felt cut off from actors and audience, as indeed she was.

Her office was never vacated except for the opera leads. For many years the opera was her first-born and dearest to her heart. The Shakespeare company was her child too, though born the wrong side of the blanket ; but that attitude of mind changed later—one of the mainsprings of Lilian Baylis's success was her ability to change her mind.

The dressing-room I used was, I suppose, the only principal men's room. It was longish and, if my memory is correct, built of rough un-whitewashed wood. The walls bulged with hanging costumes and the long bench was covered with crêpe hair, towels, spirit-gum bottles and all the untidy tangle of an actor's make-up. I am sure the room was clean but it felt dirty. It reminded me of the first dressing-room I ever occupied, when I joined the Benson company at the Theatre Royal, Belfast, in 1898. It was under the stage and none of us taller ones could stand up unless we guided our heads between the joists of the floor above. It smelt of old size and other untraceable odours ; but what did I care ? I was in a real theatre !

Sandwiched between Lilian Baylis's office and the slip dressing-rooms was a smaller office. I asked Evelyn Williams what it was called. She said she did not think it had a name, but that ' The Pigsty ' would do. (Muriel Ellis was, I believe, the secretary before Evelyn Williams.)

Irene Beeston, who worked at the Old Vic from 1920 in a literary capacity and did the Press work, has described the office as a room ten feet by eight feet. It housed Lilian Baylis's secretary, the treasurer, the producer, the girl who checked the tax vouchers, and Miss Beeston herself. It was risky to open a window as a decayed cabbage might come through it, and the door could not be opened during performances because the noise of the typewriters could be heard on the stage. ' As the last comer,' Miss Beeston writes, ' I often had my machine on the upturned wastepaper basket.' From here, too, the opera chorus were refreshed with buns and coffee in the intervals !

The crowd girls dressed in the old saloon bar and had to pass through the back of the circle to the stage. The boys used the topmost boxes and one of them has recalled in later life his embarrassment at having to run the gauntlet of some of the audience when he had to make a change in the middle of a play. That boy was John Gielgud.

There was one cold tap in the prompt corner and an adjacent gas ring which, for many of us, has immortal fame. It was here that Lilian Baylis fried her chops and tomatoes, adding an atmosphere to the dying stanzas of many a Tristan or a Romeo. Directly opposite Lilian Baylis's office, the gas ring and the sink, was the only ladies' lavatory, so it required no little strategy to effect a discreet entrance—a matter of more moment then than it is today. On one historic occasion a certain illustrious person desired to visit it. A guard of honour was hastily formed consisting of a factotum named Nightingale and two firemen. Regarding the factotum with a critical eye Lilian Baylis said, ' You had better turn your backs when she comes '—which they did.

There was no scene dock or carpenter's shop. All scenery had to be painted on the stage or at the back of the gallery. The only time the stage was empty was at night, so, often enough, the work had to be done after the play.

' Supposing anyone were to put the Old Vic of 1920 into a work of fiction,' writes Miss Beeston, ' it would be said, " No theatre ever was or could be run like that." '

HAMLET'S LITTLE JOKE
A postcard appeal of 1922.

IV

Robert Atkins

WAY back in 1915 a young actor joined the company when it was being directed by Ben Greet. He seems to have collared some good parts for himself, notably Richard III, Iago, and the one with which his name is closely associated, Sir Toby Belch. He worked at the Old Vic until he became a soldier, and presently found himself in Palestine. One day he was wondering what kind of future lay in store for him when the war ended. Being in a gloomy frame of mind he saw himself maimed and no longer able to act, and began to consider the possibilities of production. To pass the time and to divert his thoughts from death and destruction he sat down and wrote a long letter to Lilian Baylis expressing his ideas on the way Shakespeare should be played and even giving a list of possible plays for an imaginary season. The letter was signed Robert Atkins.

When he was appointed producer at the Old Vic in 1920 that dream-list of plays became, with few exceptions, a fact.

I think there is no doubt that under Robert Atkins's direction the stage work began definitely to move forward and upward. Originally all forms of entertainment sponsored by Emma Cons and Lilian Baylis were put on with the idea of filling the leisure of the half-educated masses who had but a few pence to spare from the weekly budget. To a certain extent the two women succeeded ; but now cultural ideals were being aimed at, and schools, students, and city workers of both sexes who had a taste for opera and a longing for romance and beauty found their way to the Old Vic.

The work that Robert Atkins got through between 1920 and 1925 is a colossal monument to any man's industry; but when it is remembered that it was always done in the face of daily difficulties and frustrations —for which no blame attaches to anyone—his perseverance and vitality must have had the backing of extremely sound glandular activity ! It was during these seasons that the Old Vic won the bay leaves for

ROBERT ATKINS
Producer at the Old Vic, 1920-5.

presenting every play in the First Folio. Atkins himself covered every one except *Cymbeline*. He was responsible for two plays by contemporary poets—Laurence Binyon's *King Arthur*, with music by Elgar, who conducted on the first night, and Gordon Bottomley's *Britain's Daughter*. He did a version of *Faust* translated by Tristan and Graham Rawson. I believe this was the first textually correct version presented in England. Other plays included *Everyman*, Barrie's *Pantaloon*, *Wat Tyler* (Halcott Glover), the Sheridan and Goldsmith comedies, and *A New Way to Pay Old Debts*. Lest a too-well-informed historian is getting out pen and paper to correct me let me hasten to say that I am purposely dealing with two other plays a little later.

An important event occurred in the June of 1921. The Old Vic company was invited by the Belgian Ministry of Fine Arts to appear in Brussels at the *Théâtre Royal du Parc*. It was a high honour because they were asked as representatives of the English Theatre. Of course Lilian Baylis went with them, writes Ernest Milton, ' as a hen with her chickens'. Somewhere I have read that she was missing at an important official reception but arrived before the end in a very unconventional dress, her hat awry over a flushed face, exclaiming that she had climbed to the top of the Waterloo Memorial, and could she have a wash and brush up. Perhaps she felt the Memorial was a near relative that should be called upon.

If I have any definite dislike it is for financial figures or any attribute of arithmetic beyond the White Queen's knowledge of subtraction, and therefore I do not propose to explain how sufficient money was raised round about 1923-4 to settle Morley College in its new premises in the Westminster Bridge Road and incorporate the vacated premises with those of the Old Vic. This meant decent dressing-rooms, a paint room, a carpenter's shop, offices, and many other stage advantages without which the opera and Shakespeare companies had struggled for some forty years.

The spectre of Balance—on the wrong side—continually hovered between Miss Baylis's desk and the Governors' meeting. This crisis was not the result of bad management but the demands of the L.C.C. I think there was an appeal fund which was insufficient to foot the bill, and then at the stroke of twelve a fairy godmother disguised as Sir George Dance stumped up the famous thirty thousand pounds and saved the Old Vic.

During the alterations it was proposed to send the company to a West End theatre. At first the management met with no success until Mr C. B. Cochran offered a season at the New Oxford Theatre on ' most generous terms'. It was the year of the Wembley Exhibition and it was thought that crowds of Americans and other visitors would flock to the theatres in the evening. That thought was a delusion. It turned out to be a fine, hot June and the crowds flocked to Wembley. The first performance was filled with the regular audience from the Waterloo Road but the second night the ' house' was £35. The takings, however, steadily improved during the season and Mr Cochran put, not money in his purse, but another feather in a cap already plumed with enterprising achievements. Coronations, Royal Weddings, Exhibitions and the like are never good for theatre business. Writing

ERNEST MILTON
As Hamlet in 1925. He made the first of his many appearances
with the Old Vic company in 1918.

to Bernard Shaw of the Queen Victoria Diamond Jubilee in 1897,
Ellen Terry says, 'We thought we didn't do at all well with *Sans-Gêne*
during last season, but we did far far and far away better than any
other theatre in London during that dreadful Jubilee Time.'

It was not until I went to the Old Vic to see *Henry VIII* that I was
able to taste the quality of Robert Atkins as a producer. The influence
of William Poel was evident in the simple stage settings and the swiftness
of the action. By then a substitute apron stage had been devised by
constructing a permanent false proscenium of black velvet with a
couple of doors in each pediment. Thus the plays could be staged
more or less on the Elizabethan plan. But however cleverly we scheme,
the modern 'picture frame' theatre defeats all efforts to recapture the

effect of the long entrance on which Shakespeare planned so many effects.

The false proscenium stood for a number of years, collecting the dust of time, until Tyrone Guthrie had it demolished. No doubt he was right, and the opera company had always disliked it. Guthrie had a good deal more money to spend than the early pioneers and did not have to distract his energies in trying to make old stock scenery look different.

Robert Atkins played Cardinal Wolsey. He looked the part and acted well, but I have never found the Cardinal a very exciting character. Perhaps I have yet to see the ideal Wolsey. But for an ill stroke of fortune I should have seen Irving in the part when I was twelve. Nine years later I was in the cast when Ellen Terry played Katharine at Stratford-on-Avon—an experience never to be forgotten. Florence Saunders played the Queen at the Old Vic that night, but I cannot remember her. Ion Swinley played Buckingham. I suppose few actors could fail in such a part—what good short parts Shakespeare can give us !—but Swinley was a fine actor in any part. He did much good work at the Old Vic and I was lucky to see what may have been the last part he played there—the Button Moulder in Cass's revival of *Peer Gynt*. He achieved a strange beauty that was nearer to an ethereal being than anything I have ever seen. I recall my first vision of him as a very young man bursting into a lunch party of John Drinkwater's. He was loaded with books and manuscripts, his lambent large eyes flashing with enthusiasm. What ' interfered ' with his life and kept him from touching the heights ? Was it warfare ? I do not know.

If I remember rightly Atkins threw the shadow of a cross on the backcloth in *Henry VIII* and a photograph of this scene appeared in one of the illustrated papers. Basil Dean, who at that time was doing very exciting work at the St Martin's Theatre where he had installed expensive ' Fortunae ' lamps, the latest thing in stage lighting, was so intrigued by the picture that he made his way over the Thames to ask Atkins how he had obtained this beautiful effect. Atkins showed him an ordinary bulb secreted in a square tin biscuit box. The whole of the production indeed was almost on such simple lines. Black velvet curtains, and gilt arches taking the place of wings and borders, were the basis of the decoration. This alone was the witchcraft that Robert Atkins used, and one remembers it as beautiful.

As a play *Henry VIII* wears exceeding thin towards the end, but there is a little crowd scene before the christening of the babe that is to be Queen Elizabeth, and in it the part of the porter stood out a mile as being extremely good. It was played by Hay Petrie. Someone told

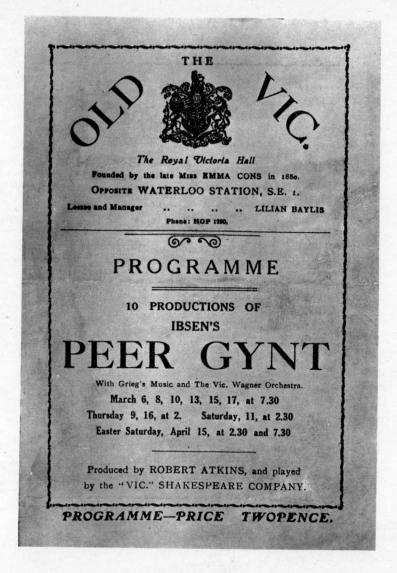

'PEER GYNT'
The first public performance in England of Ibsen's play took place at the Old Vic in March 1922, with Russell Thorndike in the title role. Robert Atkins was the producer.

me that Petrie once gave an inimitable performance as Robin the ostler in a production of Marlowe's *Dr Faustus*, and in the scene where Robin has stolen the Doctor's conjuring book and promises his friend that if he has a mind to her he shall have 'Nan Spit, our kitchenmaid . . .' he seemed to people the theatre with naked wenches.

I have inferred that Robert Atkins was influenced by the ideas of

William Poel. Later in his career he was to aim at giving a series of Shakespearean productions on a stage built as near as was possible to the one in use at the Globe in the dramatist's day. Believing as I do in the rightness of the Elizabethan method I am yet not sure that a slavish copy of it would be successful, for, even if every stage detail were correctly reproduced, there would not be the same tempered audience—the picture palace has seen to that—nor could the modern actor cope with a three-dimensional stage without special training. And again, it depends a little on the play. Of a performance of *The Tempest* at the Mansion House by the Elizabethan Stage Society in 1897, Bernard Shaw writes :

'Mr Poel says frankly, " See that singers' gallery up there ! Well, let's pretend that it's a ship." We agree ; and the thing is done. . . . But the Elizabethan method would not do for a play like *The White Heather* . . . If Mr Poel, on the strength of the Drury Lane dialogue, were to leave us to imagine the singers' gallery to be the bicycling ring in Battersea Park, or Boulter's Lock, we should flatly decline to imagine anything at all.'

Besides introducing the false proscenium of black velvet, Atkins encouraged Lilian Baylis to found a wardrobe. It cannot be too clearly stated that up to the autumn of 1933 there was very little money to spend on scenery. The existing flats and cloths were painted and repainted until the canvas sagged with the weight of the paint. There were certain rostrums which were enough to make up what was called the false stage—so that Ophelia's grave, for instance, could be suggested—and there were a few sets of steps. All these had to be used over and over again, the producer racking his brains to discover different ways of using them. It was seldom that a new back-cloth was ordered or new curtains made. Most of the stuff had to be shared with the opera company and nothing was more maddening than to find that the special item one wanted was earmarked for the other company.

Among the list of players who worked under Atkins, other than those I have already mentioned, we find the names of George Hayes, Austin Trevor, Francis L. Sullivan, Hilton Edwards, and John Laurie, who, I believe, spoke his first line on the Old Vic stage. The actresses were Marie Ney, Florence Buckton, Dorice Fordred and Jane Bacon. The Annual Report issued this year by the Governors speaks of Florence Saunders whose death had occurred during the season : ' Her death was a deep personal grief not only to the company and the staff but to many hundreds of the audience. She was particularly the Vic's own, more than any other actress except Sybil Thorndike.' Andrew Leigh

ANDREW LEIGH AND HAY PETRIE
As 'The Dromios' in *The Comedy of Errors*, 1920-1.

returned to the fold in 1924, and Ernest Milton seems to have made frequent brief returns, more than once at a time of crisis, with generous *esprit de corps*, in answer to an S O S from Lilian Baylis, who always held him dear.

Robert Atkins introduced Strindberg's *Advent* to this country and also found time to turn his attention to the opera productions—notably Dame Ethel Smyth's *The Boatswain's Mate*, Nicholson Gatty's *Tempest*, Professor Dent's new translation of *Don Giovanni*, and *Tristan and Isolde*. Atkins tells me that the singers did not see eye to eye with him over the last. To quote the words of Hilaire Belloc, 'that gives me no surprise'. A celebrated choreographer once told me that producing an opera was like trying to move a grand piano about the stage by oneself. All the same I often wish that Gordon Craig had tackled a Wagnerian opera in his early style of gigantic borderless scenery dwarfing the figures to a pleasant indistinctness.

With my own experiences in mind, I cannot conceive how Atkins found the time to include these opera jobs in his timetable. But the most important laurels that he won were without a doubt for the production, in the spring of 1922, of Henrik Ibsen's *Peer Gynt*, with Grieg's music. He got it put on in the face of great opposition. It was the first time the play had been given in a public theatre in England, and, considering the wide scope of the drama and the limited resources of the Old Vic, it was a bold undertaking. I should like to quote some observations by Bernard Shaw on *Peer Gynt*. From Paris in November 1896, where he had attended a production of the play at the *Théâtre de la Nouveauté*, he writes :

> 'The humiliation of the English stage is now complete. Paris, that belated capital which makes the intelligent Englishman imagine himself back in Dublin or Edinburgh of the eighteenth century has been before us in producing *Peer Gynt* . . . we have had the translation in our hands for four years ; and we may confidently expect the first performance in 1920 or thereabouts with much trumpeting of the novelty of the piece and the daring of the manager. *Peer Gynt* will finally smash anti-Ibsenism in Europe, because Peer is everybody's hero.'

Bernard Shaw was only two years out !

Russell Thorndike was Peer and it is quite clear that he was a real success. When in later years William Devlin came to play the part, Lilian Baylis found it difficult to accept him after Russell. 'You see Russell *is* Peer Gynt,' she said to his sister, 'a born romancer, isn't he, but I dare say William Devlin being Irish, is a bit of a romancer too—their truth is different to ours !'

The performance attracted enormous audiences and had a remarkable 'press'. Sybil Thorndike in her 'Lilian Baylis' book says that 'John Gielgud and Harcourt Williams put the Old Vic on the map of the world.' John and I may have coloured it in (J. G. by the way walked on as a young man in this production), but I believe it was Robert Atkins and his production of the Ibsen play with Russell Thorndike in the title role that drew the firm outlines of the map and imprinted a red mark on it opposite Waterloo Station.

V

Personalities and Powers

So many people are woven into the complicated pattern of the Old Vic that it is difficult to keep track of them or even to number them. Some are players, some designers, and many, such as those praised in the forty-fourth chapter of Ecclesiasticus, 'have no memorial'. Some come and go away and come again, not once but many times, as did Beatrice Wilson. Lilian Baylis, speaking once of Beatrice Wilson, said that she was the grandest woman and the grandest actress, and, ' It's her character that makes her the grandest actress '.

Miss Wilson was one of the early arrivals at the Old Vic in the days of Ben Greet, but like many another she came and went through the seasons. She once described her early experiences for a book I was editing and I feel that I cannot do better than tell them in her own words.

'Ben Greet met me at the old stage door and led me past two cubby holes, the only women's dressing rooms, to a third slightly larger cubby hole, the office. . . . A sturdy peasant woman was writing at a desk. She turned and looked at me squarely in the eyes. I noticed her crooked mouth, her pleasant face and pretty soft brown hair. " I know very little about Shakespeare," she began, " but Ben Greet tells me he wants you for those girls who dress up as boys . . . he's got to have whom he wants because he's a difficult man, you know. Sybil's used to him, but she is going to have a baby. I'll give you the same money, £2 a week. Can't pay any more. Business isn't good for Shakespeare, not like my opera. Do you believe in God? . . . All right, you'll do. Don't give yourself leading lady airs. We're democratic here."

'In spite of this strange interview,' goes on Miss Wilson, 'I took to her at once and started to form a friendship that lasted twenty-two years. The work was an ordeal. Dress rehearsals often took place on the same day as the first night and one barely had time to change from the last act dress into the first before the play began. I had

MRS NEWMAN
Wardrobe mistress of the Old Vic company from 1921-40.

the doubtful honour of dressing in the office with the continual interruption of people fetching programmes, tickets, and other oddments. How a large Shakespeare company ever managed to get dressed in such appalling accommodation was a mystery to me. When air-raids began the windows were boarded up. This, together with the heavy atmosphere of a gaslit theatre, added to the discomfort ; in which must be included the awful remnants of Victorian scenery, hired costumes and primitive lighting.

' I have a vivid recollection of an evening in 1916. I was working elsewhere, and had returned home to Bedford Park after a long rehearsal in town, to find my mother waiting for me with a telegram which had come some hours before. " Please play Viola to-night. Viola Tree ill. Lilian Baylis." It was twenty minutes to seven, the curtain rose at the Vic at 7.30 p.m. We were not on the phone. I rushed next door and phoned the Vic that I would come at once but that I had better play Olivia, as she entered later in the play, and Sybil Thorndike play Viola. A moment in my room to get some make-up, and a copy of *Twelfth Night*, with my mother's voice following me, " You can't go, you've had no dinner, dinner's ready . . . I know there will be an air-raid . . ." Through the dark roads I ran to the station, looked up the part in the train. At Waterloo, the station clock said 7.25 p.m. Racing down the Waterloo Road, I saw, as I neared the Vic, two burly figures silhouetted against the dim light of the open stage door. Lilian and Greet peering out. I shouted as I ran " I'm here." Instantly Lilian disappeared. Greet in his Malvolio clothes awaited me, pulled me panting up the little stairs, thrust a prayer book in my hand. . . . " You'll find the clothes in the office. Meet me up stage O.P." Faintly in the distance I heard the end of Lilian's speech . . . " Viola will be played by Sybil Thorndike and Olivia by our old friend Beatrice Wilson," and up went the curtain.

' I flung off my street clothes, pulled on the heavy Elizabethan dress—curse it—it fastened up the back. As I made up I felt hands fastening my dress, and a quiet voice saying,—" Good girl to come. Thank you ! I asked God to send you and he never lets down the Vic." As I hurried to the O.P. side, I heard my entrance cue. Greet pushed on the " attendant ladies " and as I reached him he held my hand an instant. " Get your breath, my dear." As I entered along the rostrum I saw facing me in the wings that sturdy woman smiling and silently clapping her hands. I turned and faced the audience. . . . After my scene Lilian bustled in to the office with a boiled egg and a cup of tea. " I knew you would be starving, my dear. Ellen Terry's in front. She says you're wonderful." '

I don't know whether it is Miss Wilson's telling of the story or whether it is the incident itself, but I always find it very moving. One cannot help feeling, too, a little pride that our hard training enables us actors to meet such an emergency. And may I draw attention to the point that here were two young actresses who were so well versed in their work that they could exchange two long Shakespearean parts at precisely fifty minutes' notice.

Beatrice Wilson was a fine actress and I think our theatre world was at fault in not making better use of her powers. Later she taught student classes at the Old Vic. Her grasp of technique, her sympathy with modern methods, and her firmness tempered with kindness, were of great service to the young.

I am not sure when students were first taken. The timetable was perhaps a little haphazard. They took fencing and dancing, and at night they ' walked on ' in whatever play was going. This last made up for any shortcomings in the curriculum. I know the students were a blessing to the producer as he was able to work with his extra people from the first rehearsal, instead of having to cope at the dress rehearsal with a number of people who knew little about the stage and less about the play. This sort of thing is no longer possible because of restrictions imposed quite reasonably by Actors' Equity. Nevertheless, I think the beginner gains so much by treading the boards and mixing with actors who have already mastered their craft that I wish there were some way out of the prohibition without prejudicing anyone else's livelihood.

Meeting Beatrice Wilson one day in 1942, she told me that she felt ' so tired ', which surprised me coming from such an energetic woman. At the time I put it down to war strain. But it was more than that. Early in the next year she died.

In 1921 there must be noted the definite arrival of a new secretary to Lilian Baylis. She was always referred to as ' Williams ' but to secure some more intimate identity for her in that rather extensive clan, her first names are Evelyn Mary.

She heard of the job through an agency which warned her that the work was heavy and the money bad. I can answer for the truth of the first warning. By the time I reached Waterloo Road she knew exactly how to deal with any emergency. She adored ' the lady ', as she called her, but managed her without fuss or nonsense. She was the pivot round which the complicated work of the opera and Shakespeare companies gyrated. Commonsense was her touchstone and if one went crying to her as if she were a Nanny, one got nothing more comforting than the truth. Her work, of course, was always behind the scenes—one might almost say behind closed doors. There is a poem by Austin Dobson about a

ORLANDO WHITEHEAD
Master of the Old Vic wardrobe for nearly twenty years.

EDWARD GORDON CRAIG
One of the master spirits of the age to whose inspiration the Old Vic, in common
with the European Theatre, owes so much.

certain Miss Peacock taking a curtain call. The author complains
that—

> *Her presence here but brings to mind*
> *That undistinguished crowd behind*
> *For whom life's not so rosy.*

Another personality, not one who 'worked the cataract', but one
who raised the wind, was Reginald P. P. Rowe, who became a Governor
of the Old Vic about 1920. For many years he held the post of Under-
Treasurer to Lincoln's Inn, but his interest was greatly in the theatre
and inevitably he became hopelessly entangled in the Old Vic web. I
am told that it was Estelle Stead who first conceived the idea of re-
claiming Sadler's Wells Theatre, but it was Reginald Rowe who turned
the dream into a reality—with Lilian Baylis, of course, standing stal-
wartly beside him. Later in life he was knighted, partly for his work
in connection with housing and partly for his whole-hearted and
unselfish support of the Old Vic and Sadler's Wells theatres. He was

a knight of burning enthusiasm—indeed, somewhere I have seen him described as ' our arch-optimist '—and a constant strength and encouragement to ' the lady '. At the time of the reconstruction of the stage during the summer vacation of 1923, when Morley College moved to its new building in the Westminster Bridge Road, Sir Reginald averted a major calamity. The work had not been in hand for more than a month when a baleful harpy in the shape of a builders' strike descended upon the theatre. The place was by then a mass of debris, floors had been ripped up and not replaced, worse still the roof was off and the stage and flies open to the sky, and, finally, Lilian Baylis had sailed for South Africa, partly for reasons of health and partly to explore the possibilities of some future tour for the company. The situation was indeed desperate. If the fine weather broke, serious damage would be done to the stage. The autumn season was in jeopardy. Sir Reginald, with the architect, Mr Chancellor, at once opened negotiations with the Union officials for a resumption of work. At first the prospect seemed hopeless, but later it was decided to make an exception of the theatre and put it in the same category as the hospitals. After the loss of only one week the work started again. No wonder Lilian Baylis acquired the habit of announcing forthcoming seasons with the phrase, ' It is hoped to reopen in September '.

That season did open, though a little later than was intended, and to get it open at the advertised time John Garside, Charles Marford, Roy Newlands (one of the actors), Rowland Robinson the carpenter, and his assistant ' Old Jock ', worked all night on the stage and then in the morning went over to Waterloo Station for baths. They breakfasted at the Waterloo Tavern and then went back to work until the afternoon, when they took a short rest. The curtain went up on time. That kind of voluntary co-operation in an emergency was not unusual. One did it as a matter of course. But for all that there was a touch of chivalry about it.

Rowland Robinson, better known to us as Rowley, was the son of ' Old Bob ' who had worked in the theatre for so many years and was now stage doorkeeper. Rowley was still the stage carpenter when I went to the Old Vic. Like most people there he had a great deal of character. He was full of guile and needed at times no little cajoling, but on the whole he was easy to get on with and one could always get a smile out of him at the end of an altercation. Tommy Connor, the property man, was another crusted character. What a nightmare his property room was, overflowing as it did under the stage ! Then there was Nightingale. I never fathomed his activities. He seemed to live the life of a badger. His lair was somewhere below and I fancy he shopped and cooked at times for ' the lady '.

John Garside reached the Old Vic in 1921 and was one of those responsible for the wardrobe which Miss Baylis saw was going to be more economical in the end than constant hiring.   A year later Garside was an acting member of the company and then again a combination of the two, or rather three, for he not only acted but designed the scenery and the costumes.   There was no room in the theatre for a wardrobe before the rebuilding, so Lilian Baylis took an old public house in Oakley Street.   Strange coincidence that this disciple of Emma Cons to whose mast was nailed the banner of temperance should thus reclaim a stronghold of the devil.   Mrs Newman was appointed ward-robe mistress.   Lilian Baylis engaged her on a month's notice—and with an ' If you don't like it you can go,' flung over her shoulder as a parting blessing.   Almost until the fatal bomb fell, Mrs Newman was still at the Old Vic on a month's notice.   One of the events of the year was the visit to the sales.   The great trouble was to stop her manageress from buying materials which were cheap, but which Mrs Newman knew would never be used.   There was indeed a cupboard full of materials, rolls of them, which lay there for years and were never used.   Once, just before the curtain was due to rise on *Tannhäuser*, it was discovered that the tights for two black boys who danced in the Venusberg scene were missing.   Lilian Baylis sent Mrs Newman running down Oakley Street to dive frantically into baskets in a vain search for the lost garments.   On arriving back at the theatre with head bowed against the coming storm she was met by a smiling manageress.   ' It's all right, my dear.   I've blacked them all over and put roses on their heads—and tied a loin cloth round their middles. They look fine.'

Those were lean days, and boots and shoes were subjects of daily wrangles in the opera world ; the Shakespeare company, poor foster-child, had but one pair of boots and a pair of shoes with red heels to share between the two men who played the leading parts.   ' I'm playing Richmond tonight, Orlando.   Is it the boots or the red heels ? '

The owner of that extraordinarily apposite Christian name was Mr Whitehead, master of the wardrobe for close on twenty years.   After the rebuilding and when the Oakley Street pub was given up, he occupied a long room lined with cupboards and hanging racks crowded with costumes.   Here in glass cases glimmered the ' crowns and crownets ', the jewelled belts, the royal orders, which in their day had adorned Milton, Gielgud, Olivier, Edith Evans and many another graced player when they evoked that unique, astounding thunder from the Old Vic audience.

One's appreciation of Orlando ripens in retrospect.   He organized

THE OLD VIC.

THE ROYAL VICTORIA HALL (Opposite Waterloo Station) S.E.1.
(FOUNDED BY THE LATE MISS EMMA CONS IN 1880.)
THE HOME OF SHAKESPEARE AND OPERA IN ENGLISH.
Lessee and Manager ... ... LILIAN BAYLIS

Celebration
ON THE
Eve of the Tercentenary of the
First Shakespeare Folio
Edited by John Heminge and Henry Condell.

IN THE PRESENCE OF
H.R.H. PRINCESS MARY, VISCOUNTESS LASCELLES
AND MANY DISTINGUISHED SHAKESPEARE LOVERS.

On *WEDNESDAY, NOVEMBER 7th, 1923, at 7.30*

Programme
OF THE PERFORMANCE OF
TROILUS & CRESSIDA

PLAYED BY THE VIC. SHAKESPEARE COMPANY. AND PRODUCED BY ROBERT ATKINS.

This play is the 36th and final play contained in the First Folio to be produced at the Old Vic. since the Autumn of 1914, by Mr. and Mrs. Matheson Lang, Mr. Ben Greet, Mr. George Foss, Mr. Russell Thorndike and Mr. Charles Warburton, and Mr. Robert Atkins for Miss Lilian Baylis.

This constitutes a record for any one theatre.

WILLIAMS & STRAHAN, LTD., Printers, London, S.E.1.

SHAKESPEARE TERCENTENARY CELEBRATION
Troilus and Cressida, given before a distinguished audience on November 7, 1923, completed the cycle of plays in the First Folio presented at the Old Vic since 1914.

his job with no little skill.　Anyone who has been to a fancy-dress ball will remember what a tangle of detail one costume involves.　Multiply one by two hundred and more, with much of the stuff in short supply, and do this every day, and one gets a vision of ' what belongs to a wardrobe '!　But how we all hated Orlando from time to time, and cursed him for not letting us have the tights we wanted, not appreciating the fact that Faust wanted them the same night at Sadler's Wells.　Actors in the throes of creating a new part have no interest in other people's troubles—and quite rightly !　There was a Dickensian flavour about Orlando : a jolly apple-coloured complexion, a baldish pate surrounded by curly locks, and a wheeze of a laugh.　His favourite holiday was a walking tour, and on his table were two tattered Blackwood magazines and a copy of Montaigne's *Essays*.

In the 1923-4 Annual Report I find a headline ' A REMARKABLE YEAR '.　It certainly was.　In the autumn of 1923, by producing *Titus Andronicus* and *Troilus and Cressida*, the Old Vic had in ten years given the whole cycle of the Shakespeare plays.　This achievement had never been equalled nor attempted by any other theatre.

On November 7 a celebration was held in honour of the tercentenary of the publication of the First Folio.　The Princess Royal and her husband were present.　The house for this event was sold out many weeks in advance, and when it was proposed that Her Royal Highness should be invited to attend, Lilian Baylis protested that there was not a seat in the house and that she would not suffer any of her dear audience to be turned out.　She was at last persuaded, however, to allow the box reserved for the Governors to be vacated, but expressed a hope that the Royal guests really liked Shakespeare.

As a crown to the year's work, the University of Oxford conferred upon Lilian Baylis the degree of Master of Arts, *honoris causa*.　With the exception of Her Majesty Queen Mary, this was the first honorary degree bestowed on a woman unassociated with the University.　Ever after that, at all public functions connected with the theatre such as first and last nights, Miss Baylis would come swishing on to the stage in her cap and gown, and I must say she wore them well.

In the summer of 1925 Robert Atkins brought five years of brilliant and exciting work to a conclusion with a revival of Sir Arthur Pinero's *Trelawny of the Wells*.　I understand that the author attended rehearsals. Was he still as dictatorial as in the old days ?　Dion Boucicault also had the reputation of being a martinet.　I wonder how the two got on when they worked together ?　Boucicault was the original Sir William Gower. Shaw did not like his performance.　' We would all, I believe, willingly push the stage old man into the grave upon whose brink he has been

'WAT TYLER', 1921-2

A design by Wilfrid Walter for the curtain of Robert Atkins's production of the play by Halcott Glover.

cackling and doddering as long as we can remember him.' But in the teeth of G.B.S. I remember, as a young man, being profoundly moved when Boucicault found Kean's sword in a theatrical hamper.

VI

A Merrie Andrew

THE King is dead.   Long live the King !   And so Robert the Magnificent gives way to Andrew Leigh who surely is consanguineous with Puck. Far back in 1914 Andrew Leigh read an advertisement in the *Era*, a stage newspaper since deceased, asking for actors for the Old Vic theatre. He attended an audition taken by Matheson Lang, who whispered in Lilian Baylis's ear that she would do well to take him.   After working at the Old Vic for a little he joined Matheson Lang's company and played Launcelot Gobbo in Lang's revival of *The Merchant of Venice* at the St James's, which I have already mentioned.   I was in it as Gratiano, a part I was fairly accustomed to, as I had played it with F. R. Benson, Arthur Bourchier, Arthur Phillips and Ellen Terry.

Andrew Leigh returned to the Waterloo Road as an actor in 1924, and began his work as producer in the autumn of 1925.   Besides being new himself, he had under him a new stage manager and assistant stage manager, as they were then called, and the management felt some anxiety about all this new blood.   However, their fears were groundless. Two brilliant players headed the company, Baliol Holloway and Edith Evans, and the production of *The Merchant of Venice* on the opening night heralded a record-breaking season.

Edith Evans's approach to the Old Vic had been a little tentative. She had recently appeared as Helena in *A Midsummer Night's Dream* at Drury Lane ' to the satisfaction of very few people and certainly not to my own ' she wrote, and she determined to find out how to play Shakespeare.   The Old Vic was the obvious place, but she thought that it was too pushing to write and suggest herself for a season.   In the end, however, she did, and opened as Portia.   She tells us that she could not understand at first why she could not make a contact with the audience there, until she discovered that in large-sized plays in large-sized theatres everything must be larger and simpler than she had been used to.   She

ANDREW LEIGH
Producer at the Old Vic, 1925-9.

played a fine round of parts—Rosalind, Queen Margaret, Cleopatra, Katharine, Beatrice, Mariana, and the Nurse in *Romeo and Juliet*. I did not see her Nurse then, but no doubt it was a foreshadowing of the magnificent characterization in Gielgud's production a few years later.

She seems to have twisted Lilian Baylis round her finger as far as new dresses were concerned, and, with the help of John Garside and Mrs Newman in the wardrobe, beautiful garments were evolved. Garside was one of those who came and went at the Old Vic. In this

BALIOL HOLLOWAY AND EDITH EVANS
As Angelo and Mariana in *Measure for Measure*, 1925-6.

70

particular season he scored many successes with effective settings and won particular praise from Edith Evans who has a well-known flair for what is right in theatre clothes.

That season broke down her shyness and not a few inhibitions. ' You don't seem to mind making a fool of yourself at rehearsal ' an actor said to her once. ' I haven't got time to mind,' was her answer. True enough of one who was plunging from one great classical part into another within a space of eight months. It is recorded that she never missed a performance, lost seventeen pounds in weight, and ran off and got married on her one free day. A truly momentous season ! She does not think that she made friends with the audience until the third production, which I believe was *The Taming of the Shrew*. I think that may be an understatement, if the box office can be a guide. But, of course, the Old Vic audience made it a custom not to suffer newcomers gladly. Reputations earned elsewhere carried no weight, but when the audience did come down on your side they grappled you to their hearts with hoops of steel. I think I am right in stating that except for the fortnight of the General Strike the theatre was sold out night after night.

That Christmas time Cicely Hamilton's *The Child in Flanders* was given with, strangely enough, a pantomime for which ' Andrew Leigh and others ' were responsible, and with a witty prologue by G. K. Chesterton ; but the most notable production of the season, other than Shakespeare, was Thomas Dekker's *The Shoemaker's Holiday*. The revival attracted a great deal of attention and was a very great box-office success. It was entirely Leigh's idea to do the revival and he met with no little opposition. Baliol Holloway also was against it. He hated it so much that he would frequently hurl the book of words angrily across the dressing-room, and John Garside, who shared the room, was in constant danger of a black eye. But in the end, of course, as Simon Eyre, Holloway scored highly, and Garside says that Edith Evans in the small part of the wife, Margery Eyre, did some of her best work.

Holloway's fine performance as Richard III must be known to many, as he produced it at the New Theatre five years later. I did not see his Falstaff in *The Merry Wives of Windsor* until he played the part at the Stratford-on-Avon Memorial Theatre in 1921. I thought his the best Falstaff I had seen up to that time, and, considering the litheness of his tall figure, a remarkable one from the point of view of make-up ; neither did he obscure his facial expression. Beerbohm Tree, who enjoyed a not undeserved reputation for clever make-up, went too far as Falstaff and so covered his face with padding and whiskers that it became an immovable mask.

Naturally, after the triumphant season just dealt with the following

'KING JOHN', 1926-7

Left to right : John Wyse (Dauphin), Graveley Edwards (King of France), Dorothy Massingham (Constance), John Garside (Pandulph). This was the opening production of Andrew Leigh's second season.

one was bound to show a slight declension on the graph board. Leigh was fortunate, however, in retaining the services of Baliol Holloway and many of the male members of the company. The opening play, *King John*, played to capacity audiences, which makes one surmise that Holloway's Bastard was exceptionally good, for *King John* does not rank among the more popular histories. Dorothy Massingham, daughter of the famous editor of the *Nation*, shared the leads with Gwynne Whitby, who was a daughter of a very fine Shakespearean actor, Arthur Whitby. He was a most genial soul and always kind and encouraging to the young ; but he would put up with no posing, or nonsense, and he considered the first duty of an actor was to know the author's words. He regarded the trilby hat with grave suspicion and had a rooted antipathy to long hair, and at quite an early age had extremely little of that commodity himself.

I am not one to foster superstition, but really it is very difficult to avoid the *Macbeth* hoodoo in the theatre. Holloway damaged himself in the fight this time, and Ernest Milton courageously rushed into the

72

'HENRY V', 1926-7

Centre : Baliol Holloway (Henry) and Gwynne Whitby (French Princess). Producer : Andrew Leigh. Settings and costumes were designed by John Garside, who also acted at the theatre.

breach. He had not played the part for some years and rehearsed with the iron safety curtain down while the audience was actually in the house.

A Chester Nativity play—*The Play of the Shepherds*—was revived this Christmas with a play by Rose Fyleman entitled *Christmas Eve*. I had seen the Chester Nativity play when it was done by Robert Atkins about 1925 with Hauptmann's *Hannele*. I remember it as a very lovely thing of simple, rugged humour. *Hannele*, too, I enjoyed. Swinley was the Pastor who in the child's dream seems to be Christ. According to the Annual Report the audience do not seem to have shared my appreciation of the German play. Maybe they preferred the warmer roast-goose-and-Christmas-pudding atmosphere of the Dickens *Carol* which accompanied the first appearance of the Chester Nativity play.

The following year the front of the house had to be dealt with to fulfil the demands of the L.C.C. At first it was feared that there would be no performances in the 1927-8 season, then Sir Nigel Playfair offered a home to the company at the Lyric Theatre, Hammersmith, and there

BALIOL HOLLOWAY AND NEIL PORTER
As the disguised King and Pistol in *Henry V*, 1926-7. Andrew Leigh first introduced
Baliol Holloway to Old Vic audiences.

they stayed until February 7, 1928.   Sybil Thorndike and Lewis Casson
played the leads and were supported by Hay Petrie, Mary Sumner,
Winifred Oughton, Iris Roberts, Reyner Barton and John Laurie.
The five months' season was a success and the Old Vic reopened on
Saint Valentine's day with *Romeo and Juliet*.   There was the usual last-
minute scramble which seems to accompany the opening of any theatre,
and it is said that the last nail in the stair carpet was hammered in as
the audience entered.

The Cassons went off on some other work and Ernest Milton, Baliol
Holloway and Rupert Harvey returned to the fold. Jean Forbes-
Robertson, Barbara Everest and Grace Allardyce replaced Sybil
Thorndike and the others.

The staging of *The Two Noble Kinsmen*, a play supposed by many to be
written by Shakespeare and Fletcher, aroused a good deal of interest and
Jean Forbes-Robertson distinguished herself as the Gaoler's Daughter.

Before the following season had run its course Lilian Baylis received
another honour. This time from the King. In the New Year's
Honours List of 1929, she was granted admission to the Order of the

'KING LEAR', 1927-8

Left to right : Jean Forbes-Robertson (Cordelia), Ernest Milton (Lear), Percy Walsh (Kent).   Final production of the season.

Companions of Honour.   The order was instituted in 1917 and limited to sixty-five persons.   It ranks immediately after the Grand Cross of the British Empire and before the K.B.E. and the D.B.E.   Its recipients must be subjects of the Crown who have rendered conspicuous service of national importance.   I have only recently read those words and they have opened my eyes to something I had never realized before—why Lilian Baylis was so proud of the little enamelled brooch she wore whenever she made a public appearance.   She was invested with that decoration on March 28 by H.R.H. Edward, Prince of Wales, acting for His Majesty, King George V, who was still recovering from his illness at Bognor.

Financial difficulties again swept down upon the Governors with renewed vigour.   There was the expense of rehousing Morley College, and an alarming crisis during the rebuilding of the auditorium when it was found that the condition of the structure was such that the cost would far exceed expectations.   The situation was saved for the moment by help from the Carnegie Trust, the City Parochial Foundation, and a munificent gift from Mr Harry Lloyd.   All this happened, I think, under the chairmanship of Sir Wilmot Herringham, who now resigned after eight years' service. The Governors were very fortunate in their new chairman, the Earl of Lytton. He proved an extremely able man, not only in this capacity, but also in others of a like nature, and he endeared himself to all with whom he came in contact. It was a deep loss to the Old Vic and his many friends when he died towards the end of 1947.

I first met Lord Lytton in 1907, when he presided at a dinner given for Granville-Barker and his business partner, J. E. Vedrenne, in honour of the historic season of three years at the Court Theatre, Sloane Square. I remember Lytton as a handsome, debonair young man, who spoke extremely well. Bernard Shaw had been closely concerned in the enterprise and, I presume because he was present, the Savoy gave us two menus, one ordinary and one vegetarian. Granville-Barker asserted that he had been through both menus but had enjoyed neither because he knew he was foredoomed to make an after-dinner speech. Beerbohm Tree spoke last and at such length that I missed my last train to Croydon. Lewis Casson, who was sitting by me, offered to put me up at his bachelor room in Clifford's Inn. He explained to me that he could supply nothing very luxurious in the way of a bed, but at twenty-seven that did not trouble me. However, I was somewhat aghast on arriving on the top floor of one of those lovely old buildings to find that my bed was a wooden window seat with ne'er a cushion to soften the unresisting oak. I wrapped myself in a blanket, and did not sleep a wink. In the morning Casson took me into Kenelm Foss's rooms for breakfast, and suggested that I should wash in the bedroom. To my surprise it was hung about with female garments. On coming out, Lewis, looking slightly embarrassed, hastily explained that perhaps he ought to tell me that Foss had recently made a secret marriage. Later I slunk home from East Croydon Station trying to disguise from our neighbours that I was in evening dress at eleven o'clock in the morning. But, dear me, this has nothing to do with the theatre or the Old Vic.

Had I been aware of the prospect before me I should have made it my business to attend the Old Vic performances far more frequently than I did. Much as I enjoyed producing plays I never thought of it as a whole-time occupation. As an actor, I had an unexpressed jealousy of the producer in me. I had no intention of allowing that parvenu to push aside the actor, as indeed he did for four years on end. I could not guess at those things which would be added unto me—a release, for example, from that grinding self-centredness to which we are all addicted in some degree. The act of interpreting the design and thoughts of an author whom one respects and loves, and the task of

EDITH EVANS
As Portia in *The Merchant of Venice*, during
her first season at the Old Vic, 1925-6.

JOHN LAURIE
He appeared regularly at the Old Vic from
1921 to 1925, and again from 1927 to 1929.

directing actors, some of whom are inexperienced enough to need help
and advice, tend to divert one's thoughts from self. Call it a spiritual
emancipation.

John Laurie was the leading man in this, Andrew Leigh's last, season.
I saw him as Macbeth and Hamlet; both first-rate performances.
His incisive diction, his Scottish vigour, and his warm personality are
now known to all of us.

The other plays I saw were *As You Like It* and *The Rivals* with Andrew
Leigh as an admirable Bob Acres—the first one I had ever seen
who was anywhere near the right age! The company as a whole gave
good, satisfactory performances. Esmé Church carried the leading
women's parts with all the skill and experience she had gathered with
the Lena Ashwell Players. Other players I remember particularly are
Torin Thatcher, Percy Walsh, Wilfred Babbage, and Horace Sequeira.

Harley Granville-Barker thought that the Old Vic had been over-
praised. In a sense that was true, but chiefly it was the exceptional
performances that won too florid praises. I have always felt that the
Press, and indeed the public, other than the Old Vic *habitués*, have been

strangely indifferent to the very fine work done there. The fact that much of our work enjoyed none of the comfort and organization that obtains in West End theatres, and was often brought to birth with pangs of labour, does not affect the issue. We asked for no consideration on that account. But as a repertory theatre that consistently did sound, capable work, and was equal in its ensemble to most performances across the water, the Old Vic deserved more attention and genuine respect than were usually accorded it.

The management expected me to decide, before the end of the season, which of the present company I intended to retain, and I was forced to consider the work with a critical eye. I felt that the tempo was on the whole too slow and that too much time was wasted on stage business often of a traditional nature. I also thought that owing to the construction of the false proscenium the action of the play was frequently thrown too far up-stage. As for the players themselves I would gladly have asked some of them to join my banner, but I knew that it would really be wiser to start with a clean slate ; in a way this must have been a sign of weakness in me, as I should have felt confident that given a good actor I could have moulded him to my way of thinking.

Andrew Leigh ventured boldly in his non-Shakespearean productions. He produced *Adam's Opera* by Clemence Dane, with music by Richard Addinsell, for which he had the great advantage of securing the services of Marie Löhr. There was an Ibsen centenary revival of *The Vikings*. Gordon Craig did a production of this for his mother at the Imperial Theatre in 1903, and I was there on the first night. The scene of the banqueting hall was one of the most exquisitely beautiful stage settings I have ever seen—a great circular dais beneath a lovely corona of lights, and vast towering walls that disappeared in the blue mystery of the roof tree. Leigh also put on a revival of Robertson's *Caste*, made especially noteworthy by the playing of Madame Rachel Berendt of the *Odéon*, Paris, in the role of Esther. As a granddaughter of the author, her appearance called for a great gathering of the Robertson clan on the first night, among them Dame Madge Kendal (Robertson's young sister). Finally, there was Maeterlinck's *Mary Magdalene*, which took the place of the perennial *Everyman* with much success.

The Annual Report devotes a very long paragraph to the departure of Andrew Leigh. It seems that the most important thing he did was to instigate and produce Dekker's *The Shoemaker's Holiday*, which met with such triumphant success. There are two little sentences in the Report which tells us a great deal . . . ' They were four of the most peaceful and untroubled years the Old Vic has ever experienced ', and, ' He never lost the friendship and goodwill of a single one of those who have worked with him.'

VII

My Watch

ONE morning in March 1929 I received a letter from Lilian Baylis offering me the post of producer of plays. At first I was not particularly interested. The actor in me rebelled. But in course of time my attitude changed and I took on the responsibility with enthusiasm. I remained ' four years at the Old Vic ', and in a book bearing that title I have told of my experiences in some detail. At the time I think I worried too much, especially during the early weeks of my first season. Now, time—that illusive and on the whole kind parent—has obliterated some of the worse moments. In many ways fortune favoured me. I had John Gielgud and Martita Hunt, both then unknown to a wide public, for my leads. Such men as Granville-Barker, John Masefield, William Poel and Gordon Craig, if not actually backing me, were certainly very much on my side. I had, too, the penetrating criticism of an expert artist in the person of my wife, criticism that was always tempered with judicious encouragement.

My single purpose at the beginning was to restore the pace to Shakespeare plays not only in the speaking of the verse but in the movement of the scenes. Ever since the 'nineties, Poel had been demanding this, and Granville-Barker before the 1914 war had achieved it. I overdid it at first and brought down an avalanche on my head from Press and public. I thought that my heart, like Bloody Mary's, would be inscribed—with ' Shakespeare gabbled ' ! However, in a very short time the company learned how to combine speed with rhythm and audibility. It took longer for them to weld themselves into a reasonable ensemble— six or eight weeks I should say. The theatre was still shared with the opera and in those days we acted on Monday, Wednesday and Friday nights, Thursday afternoons, and alternate Saturday afternoons. We had three weeks to rehearse a play—which on paper does not seem too bad—but we were often unable to use the stage because it was wanted by the carpenters and scene painters and so forth, and the rehearsal room at the top of the building was large but an awkward shape as a substitute for the stage.   The acoustics in the rehearsal room were not too good, and when a large company is herded into one room there are bound to be disturbances.   The three nights off a week were a great boon to the actors and gave them time to learn their words.

Up to my day Lilian Baylis always welcomed the company with a short address.   Some who scarcely knew her and judged her by hearsay were inclined to snigger inwardly at the homeliness of her approach, but it did stress the point that we were all one family for the next nine months, to stand or fall together.

Our first play was *Romeo and Juliet*.   John Gielgud's Romeo has been seen since at its most brilliant.   Then, it was perhaps the least interesting thing he did, but that does not mean that it was at any point less good. Adèle Dixon, an enchanting Juliet, has made her name in other spheres. The success of the acting (as far as I was concerned) was Martita Hunt's Nurse—a hot-tempered, vulgar Italian peasant and young enough to have suckled Juliet whatever her tender years may have been.   Very difficult those ages !   Juliet but fourteen and the nurse with only four teeth in her head !   There had been a conventional attitude to age in the theatre right up to the 1914 war.   Mothers were expected to be grey-locked and fathers grey-bearded no matter how young their children might be.   Clearly the Elizabethan playwrights still used the traditions from earlier forms of drama.

The Merchant of Venice followed, and this met with no greater approval. How well I remember the cast hiding the newspapers which contained the worst notices as I drew near them !   They must have been bad, because I was so overwhelmed by an inferiority complex that I virtually tendered my resignation to Lilian Baylis.   That was my first insight into that remarkable woman's character.   I don't think it was so much what she said to me at that interview as the way she said it.   Something told me beyond doubt that she had faith in me, and that sense never left me.

I suppose physically and nervously I was suffering from the strain of starting on such a stupendous task and getting two productions under way.   But I was soon to get my second wind and I had a letter of great encouragement from Max Plowman.   He liked *The Merchant of Venice* and thanked me for restoring the balance of the play.   Max Plowman, poet, and student of Blake, wrote some extremely illuminating essays on some of Shakespeare's plays.   He died too early.

One sometimes remembers with surprise that Antonio is the title role in *The Merchant of Venice*.   Gielgud played him with real sympathy and

HARCOURT WILLIAMS
Producer at the Old Vic, 1929-33.

distinction. The Shylock of Brember Wills was right enough but not up to the standard of his own capabilities, which I, and others, thought had a touch of genius in them. Young Donald Wolfit as Lorenzo spoke the verse in the last act exquisitely.

I had a good few heartening letters about that time, in particular one from Harley Granville-Barker. He had found time to see a little of the play and sent me some very useful criticisms and certain praise, which, coming from a master, was not inconsiderable.

Sir Barry Jackson introduced me to a version of Molière's *Le Malade Imaginaire* written by F. Anstey, the author of *Vice Versa*. I persuaded the management to let me do it as a change from the usual old English comedies of Goldsmith and Sheridan which had become something of a commonplace in the repertoire. I used Mozart's *Eine Kleine Nachtmusik* for incidental music. Each character had its musical theme and some of the dialogue and business was done in time to it. We wound up the play with a heavenly hornpipe of Purcell's. Some of the critics accused me of imitating the methods of Sir Nigel Playfair at the Lyric Theatre, Hammersmith—his work at that theatre was then very much the vogue—but this was sheer nonsense. If I was imitating anyone it was Margaret Morris and the work she did at her miniature theatre in Flood Street, Chelsea, and the ideas of Jean Sterling Mackinlay and her children's matinees which sprang in their turn from Froebel's teaching.

Anstey came to quite a few rehearsals and like many comic spirits he was a shy, reserved little man. The play fitted the company like a glove, from Brember Wills as the Invalid to Margaret Webster who held it together as Toinette. John Gielgud and Adèle Dixon sang the music lesson with just the right touch of burlesque, and Martita Hunt hid her money in her garter with admirable Parisian suggestiveness.

By the time he had reached *Richard II* Gielgud was an established favourite. I can see now that my production of that play was influenced in some degree by my recollection of what we did in the Benson company. The Benson company, I may say, was big enough to borrow from (Granville-Barker said that of Gordon Craig), and at its height all the managers in London were falling over each other to lure actors and actresses away from it. Frank R. Benson (Sir Frank Benson) who founded the company often played the King magnificently. In my time I have seen some half a dozen Richards. Some shone in other ways than John Gielgud's brilliance in the part, but none have touched his poetic imagery and emotional power.

I think I am right in saying that the play drew full houses, but Lilian Baylis would never permit me to see the ' returns ' so I can only guess.

MARTITA HUNT AND JOHN GIELGUD
As Gertrude and Hamlet, 1929-30.

This was ever a bone of contention. Undoubtedly the producer in such an organization should know exactly how the public is responding to his efforts. Until shortly before she died Lilian Baylis held the end of every string in her hand and for that one cannot blame her ; one can only bow one's head in admiration of her administrative ability.

All I could do was to wander into the box office and look over the booking plans with Mrs Clark.

The reviews of *Richard II* were not too favourable, and I had a note from Beatrice Wilson saying among other things, ' The Press are swine-faced rats ! You should have had magnificent notices.'

However, the next effort won them over entirely. We had magnificent notices and packed houses. The play was *A Midsummer Night's Dream*. We made a Jacobean masque of it inspired by Inigo Jones, and Paul Smyth our designer painted a glorious wood with a sky of silver. I threw Mendelssohn overboard, and used the arrangement of English country airs put together by Cecil Sharp for the Granville-Barker production in 1914 at the Savoy. This caused no end of a sensation in the last ditches of the Lower Marsh and letters of protest rained upon me. I had had my bellyful of these in my early days. They were generally anonymous and therefore unanswerable, but my withers were unwrung. One letter, I remember, complained that the writer had been used to telling her friends that when she took them to see *A Midsummer Night's Dream*, she took them to an opera as well as a play—on the principle of two treats for the price of one I suppose !

Professor Dent, in his book *A Theatre for Everybody*, did not like the innovation and I respect the point of view of so distinguished a musician, but on the other hand such an eminent critic as Desmond MacCarthy still considered, in 1948, that the Savoy productions of *Twelfth Night* and *A Midsummer Night's Dream* were the most lovely performances of Shakespeare he had ever seen.

I was well served by my actors over this production. Gielgud and Adèle Dixon were the Oberon and Titania, and Margaret Webster, Donald Wolfit, Francis James, and Martita Hunt played their scenes—scenes which can be so dull—in a vein of high comedy. I have a belief that one day Martita Hunt will startle the commercial manager as a great comedienne. We had a newcomer too, to play Puck : Leslie French. I have known him since he was a boy and watched his career with interest and delight. He stayed with me until the end of my second season and from the first moment he appeared as Puck the Old Vic audience took him to their hearts.

I had an awkward moment with Lilian Baylis over this play. I was going my rounds of the dressing-rooms on the first night and found her

The Old Vic

FOUNDED BY THE LATE MISS EMMA CONS IN 1880.

WATERLOO ROAD S.E.1.

BOX OFFICE TELEPHONE—HOP 3424, 3425.

Lessee and Manager - - LILIAN BAYLIS, CH., M.A., Oxon. (Hon.

SEASON, 1930-31.

OPENING NIGHT OF SHAKESPEARE SEASON
SATURDAY, SEPT. 13, at 7.45

HENRY IV. (Part I.)

Also Monday, Wednesday and Friday, Sept. 15, 17, 19, 22, 24, 26, 29,
Oct. 1 and 3, at 7.45

Thursday, Sept. 18, 25, and Oct. 2, at 2.30

Saturday, Sept. 20, and Oct. 4, at 2.30

PLAYED BY THE VIC SHAKESPEARE COMPANY.

Programme—Price THREEPENCE

' HENRY IV, PT I '

The opening production of the 1930-1 season. Ralph Richardson as Prince Hal made his Old Vic debut. John Gielgud appeared as Hotspur.

85

sitting in the girls' dressing-room. As I came in she let slip something detrimental to the production. My condition was one of extreme anxiety as to how my work was going to be received and I felt quite justly that she should not pass judgement on it in front of the company. I lost my temper. I don't remember what I said but I know I regretted it within ten minutes. I apologized and that was the end of that.

Fairly early in the season the L.C.C. matinees began. I can't remember how many we did in the season but they were an added tax on our timetable. The Council took the theatre for an afternoon and it was packed with children of all ages. I was told that it had been the custom to let the understudies play at these matinees, but I was against the notion that the second-best would do for children and I arranged for the usual performances to be given. This put an added strain on the leading people, as playing to that type of audience requires a special technique. I used to talk to the children before we started just to give them some idea of what to expect and to put non-cinema ideas into their heads about kissing. That manoeuvre was a success. They had of course had the ' books ' of the play in class, but at that time Shakespeare was still being made a bogey of in all schools. I am told that now the Council schools act the plays in class, which fills me with hope.

It was in vain that I tried to get the L.C.C. to choose at least one unfamiliar play for the children to see. Such an innovation was looked upon as a ' joy-ride '. One of the masters, speaking of *The Tempest*, once said to me, ' This is quite a humorous play. One does not think of Shakespeare as humorous.' But I really believe that the era of the teacher's love of notes and anachronisms is passing away, and the poetry, emotion, and drama of the plays are getting a look in at last.

Another drain upon our time and energy were the ' functions '. There was always some tea party or social gathering cropping up which had become a tradition in the prehistoric days and had been of great use in the development of an audience, when there was no money to spend on publicity in the usual way. There was a parochial flavour about these affairs which the actors found irksome. Although the private life of a player is now generally better known than his work in the theatre, as a race we do not like parading before an audience out-side the mystery of our art, to be stared at like animals in a circus. (Animals don't like it either.) At the cutting of the cake on Twelfth Night the company in their costumes used to make a progress in procession from the stage right round the full auditorium and back again. Lilian Baylis would then cut the cake and it would be handed round with glasses of lemonade to the audience. All this was too much to ask of leading players who had been rehearsing all day and acting long parts at night, and had an inevitable rehearsal next morning. The ceremony of the cake and any high jinks on the stage ending with everyone joining hands and singing *Auld Lang Syne*—that is good fun, and is what we have now arrived at, anyway at Sadler's Wells.

It was in 1927 that Granville-Barker published the first volume of his *Prefaces to Shakespeare*. The one on *Julius Caesar* fired me with an ambition to do the play on his lines. After Christmas the opportunity occurred. John Gielgud was cast as Antony, Martita Hunt as Portia, Donald Wolfit as Cassius, and Gyles Isham as Brutus. At least, that was my best-laid scheme—but it went agley. One weekend Gyles Isham fell from his horse and broke his collarbone. It was within a few days of production, and there was nothing for it but for me to take on the part. I knew all the moves, and the rest of the work was practically finished.

On the first night I was on my way to the stage for my first entrance when I met Lilian Baylis. Many stories have been told of her famous gaucheries. One is lost to the world. She said something to me at that moment so devastating that had I not been past consciousness of anything but my grim determination not to let my colleagues down I should have been shattered. The odd thing is that what she said to me has passed for ever from my mind. Come to think of it, she who lived under a constant nervous strain must have felt the additional pull of a first night with the rest of us, although she might not admit it. What is it M'Comas says in *You Never Can Tell*?—'There are men who have a good deal of feeling and kind feeling too, which they are not able to express . . . Think of the people who do kind things in an unkind way—people whose touch hurts, whose voices jar, whose tempers play them false, who wound and worry the people they love in the very act of trying to conciliate them, and yet need affection as much as the rest of us.'

The pseudo-classic, dreamlike nature of *A Midsummer Night's Dream* permits one to indulge in any kind of extravagance, but anyone who attempts anything in the way of realism in devising a set for the Forest of Arden will certainly come a cropper.

Occasional stretches of open country are found scattered about great forests, and for *As You Like It* we decided to have two or three solid tree trunks in the foreground and vistas of undulating country beyond, cultivated to some extent by the farming fraternity—the shepherds, Corin, Silvius and Phebe, and Audrey with her goats. Gyles Isham was still away so Baliol Holloway came back to play Jaques, a part he took in his stride with distinction.

LESLIE FRENCH AS ARIEL
In the productions of *The Tempest*, 1930-1 and 1932-3.

When I suggested in the office that I should ask Bernard Shaw for *Androcles and the Lion* and *The Dark Lady of the Sonnets*, I sensed a kind of shimmer in the air—like the heat mirage that hovers above the road surface after a shower. I don't suppose Lilian Baylis cared two raps about the Irishman's tilting at Bardolatry, but she thought he would not let us have the plays, and she possibly remembered the Governors' attitude to *Candida* fifteen years ago. The upshot was that Shaw sent us the necessary licences.

The part of Shakespeare in *The Dark Lady of the Sonnets* is a fascinating one. I played it at the London Coliseum with Haidée Wright as Queen Elizabeth for two or three weeks. How she hated the part and how good she was in it! Holding that vast auditorium during the long speech to the Queen was a thrilling adventure. When I played the part again at the Old Vic I had a superb audience for all the Shakespeare quotations!

The double bill hit the target bang in the middle as far as business went. John Gielgud made an eccentric dilettante of the Emperor, and Martita Hunt's stark honesty as Lavinia was a fine foil to John Wyse's Handsome Captain. This of course was a return visit of Wyse to his old home. I think Androcles was the best thing Brember Wills did, and the situation at the end of the prologue when he dances away with the Lion to the Blue Danube Waltz, leaving his scold of a wife behind, was a moment of real grotesque comedy which I seldom missed watching. Inside the Lion's skin was Richard Ainley, Henry Ainley's son, and, being a born actor, his gesture and whole carriage could not have been bettered. Richard came to me as a very young man, full of enthusiasm and extremely intelligent and cultured. It was a delight to watch his skill and personality developing like some rare flower.

For me the most enthralling play from a producer's point of view is *Macbeth*. It is so well designed, so swift of action, and so compact. There is nothing extraneous at all if one deletes the obvious interpolations of Hecate and the English doctor. Gielgud was twenty-seven years old at the time of this production and with a physique that did not suggest the brawny Scot of theatrical tradition ; but with skilful dressing and make-up, his Macbeth was a fine enough figure and he played it exquisitely. Unless my judgement is prejudiced I do not think he has bettered that performance and it was, in my opinion, the best thing that he did at that time. Martita Hunt as Lady Macbeth was no mean consort. The care bestowed on productions far more richly caparisoned, and cast with a lavish disregard of finance, did not add one iota to the integrity of Gielgud's performance in this play or in any other.

Maurice Jacobson supplied the incidental music. His dramatic instinct is unfailing and one wishes he would let the theatre make more use of it. Paul Smyth with the little at our disposal contrived some handsome stage pictures and Peter Watts lit them to perfection.

Our last hurdle was *Hamlet*. It had become a tradition that the play should be given two or three performances in its entirety as well as some performances with the usual cuts at the end of the season. The full version running nearly five hours with one break of half an hour proved more popular than the short one, and always drew full houses. A distinguished critic (Ivor Brown, I believe) wrote that the less that is cut of *Hamlet* the shorter it seems. I fancy most people who have once seen an ' Entirety ' do not get much satisfaction from any other version.

When deliberating on a play of Shakespeare's I have always tried to see it first as a story of today, with its situations translated into modern circumstances, and the reactions of each character in relation to them.

I used to suggest to the actors, especially the younger ones, that they should turn the dialogue into the vernacular before actually learning the verse. In *Hamlet* particularly I was anxious to express its all-time, and consequently its modern, application. After the first scene on the battlements we find ourselves inside the castle at Elsinore. I determined to abandon the customary court formalities with the King and Queen crowned, robed and enthroned in state. I placed the Queen on a balcony embroidering a length of brocade with her ladies-in-waiting. How admirably Martita Hunt did this and what a satisfactory character she made of the Queen ! I have never seen a better. Nor have I seen a better King than Donald Wolfit. He made his first entrance dressed for hunting and hurrying through the tiresome state business as quickly as possible—what a difficult young man Hamlet was to be sure ! The atmosphere was domestic first and political afterwards.

'TWELFTH NIGHT', 1931-2
Ralph Richardson as Sir Toby Belch, with Harold Chapin as Sir Andrew Aguecheek.

RALPH RICHARDSON AS DON PEDRO
In *Much Ado About Nothing*, 1930-1.

Gielgud's Hamlet has been seen many times. I have seen it three times since he first played it. In each production there has been some valuable addition, some new insight and power, but what he had at the Old Vic was youth : no merit in him I know, and he is still young enough to play the part for years, but there was an appeal in that youthful interpretation of the character that broke the heart.

Before the last night three things had happened. Lilian Baylis had re-engaged me, Maurice Browne had undertaken to transfer the whole *Hamlet* production to the Queen's Theatre and, most important of all, John Gielgud had signed a contract for the next season.

Of all the Old Vic 'functions' the last night was the most remarkable. The fall of the curtain was a signal for an indescribable scene. The

JOHN GIELGUD
As Lear, 1930-1.

whole company and staff assembled on the stage, tables loaded with gifts and flowers were carried on, and their burdens distributed. Gifts from the gallery, from the pit, and from the stalls. Rich gifts and packets of cigarettes. No one was forgotten. Lilian Baylis, supreme in her Oxford robes and with His Majesty's decoration on her breast, set the ball rolling. In the early days she did not like making speeches, and then one night when a bad raid began in War Number One, she went in front of the curtain and talked to the audience in her homely way and found it easy. At a dinner given by a women's club she spoke for over an hour. She held in her hands a bundle of notes that Evelyn Williams had prepared for her, but never once referred to them. She merely waved them about and kept her audience in fits of laughter, and yet she contrived to say everything of importance that she meant to say, including a forceful begging for the Vic-Wells fund.

On these stage appearances she seemed to me to assume another personality. There was something of the music-hall artist's approach to her audience, something of the dancing mistress and her concert work in South Africa. She always directed her looks straight up at the gallery which was not bad technique, but I always thought that she was going back to the days when the rough crowd of the gin palaces was huddled on the wooden benches. She was capable of blurting out the most original points of view. I heard her once say, ' I would rather go to a funeral than a last night of the season, because I *do* believe in the Resurrection.'

After Lilian Baylis's speech we all had to follow suit, and when at a late hour the curtain had fallen she would kiss me goodbye as if we were parting for ever, whereas, in fact, we were meeting next morning at half-past ten to get down to planning the next season.

Our *Hamlet* in Shaftesbury Avenue at the Queen's Theatre caused some sensation ; it was particularly interesting because at that time the German actor Moissi was playing the same part at the Globe next door and one was able to compare the differences of approach to the play. On the whole it was more robust than ours. I particularly recall an angry old gentleman arrayed in a winding sheet as the Ghost. It was most refreshing. We had one slight accident at the Queen's. We were using our false stage there. When the Gravedigger put his hand down for Yorick's skull he found it had rolled away because the Queen's stage had a rake to the footlights, whereas our Old Vic stage was flat. We sent round to the Globe for the German skull, but it arrived too late and John had to decide rapidly on a drastic cut in the text.

When I was sitting in the circle watching the scenery being set, Herbert Menges, who was the conductor at the Queen's, told me how much he would like to work at the Vic. As soon as Sadler's Wells was opened—and that was now imminent—Charles Corri would have to devote all his time to opera, so I suggested to Lilian Baylis that Menges should join us. He did and I think he has stayed, with the exception of the war years, ever since. I know that his coming was a great joy to me.

The new company was quite exciting. I had spotted a young actor called Ralph Richardson in Sir Barry Jackson's production of *Back to Methuselah*. By the time I wanted him he was playing Roderigo at the

'King Lear', 1930-1
Setting designed by Paul Smyth.

Savoy in *Othello*, with Paul Robeson and Peggy Ashcroft. Leslie French, George Howe and Richard Ainley stayed on and I had an influx of actors' children—Anthony Hawtrey, Valentine Dyall, Joan Harben and Harold Chapin. And then I had the good fortune to persuade Dorothy Green to join us.

The reopening of Sadler's Wells was becoming an accomplished fact by this time. Towards the end of this last season I and the stage management, heads of staff, opera producer, and electrical experts were summoned to a meeting to discuss the lighting arrangements for the as yet unfinished theatre. I must confess that I was in agreement with most of the departments that the difficulties of running the two theatres seemed insurmountable. It was Lilian Baylis and Reginald Rowe who believed wholeheartedly in the scheme—and, I expect, Ninette de Valois, who was to find in the Wells a future of exceptional brilliance. But at that time there was no ballet apart from that needed for the operas.

It was Gielgud's idea that we should open the next season with *Henry IV, Part I*. What a capital play it is to act! Gielgud and

Richardson made an astoundingly happy pair as Hotspur and Prince Hal. I shall not forget their encounter at the end of the play. On the first night Richardson was frightened to death. He brought in a bottle of champagne to give himself some dutch courage. ' I couldn't get the darned thing open,' he said afterwards. ' In desperation I knocked the neck against the edge of the table and it exploded like a Mills bomb—all over the walls—everywhere—and then you came in to wish your new leading man luck ! '

Hal was in bed for his first scene and Falstaff brought him a dish of buttered eggs and later, I think, Poins brought him his shaving water. All thoroughly on the domestic line ! We did splendid business with this play, and the whole season was pretty good in spite of a change of policy towards the end.

For *The Tempest* we decided on a Persian-cum-Japanese décor. I wrote to John Masefield about that complicated ship scene and he sent me clear and witty explanations. Prospero, who is usually made into a dull old boy by most actors, in John's sensitive hands became a being of great beauty. Ralph Richardson made a Mongolian monster of Caliban. He is a particularly clever artist in make-up and his draughtsmanship must be a great help to him.

Algernon Blackwood who admits to no great affection for Shakespeare on the stage was entirely won over by our *Tempest*. Of Leslie French's Ariel he wrote to me, ' I found it that rare thing, lovely. Ariel satisfied and I'm hard to satisfy. I shall never forget Ariel against the sky when he takes his liberty at last. Haunting.'

It was while we were playing this that Gielgud was ' off ' for two performances—the only two in two years. Our understudy arrangements were necessarily sketchy and we had no one ready to go on for Prospero. I had to read it. Peter Watts prepared a part in a kind of magic book for me which I could read without spectacles. The first time I read it so successfully that many in the audience did not know that I *was* reading, but at the second performance next day I blundered all over the place. I have often observed this kind of first-time luck in such a crisis. I suppose one has to undertake the job so suddenly that one has no time to be self-conscious. One's training and intuition have free play.

I have nothing to say about our next play except that Dorothy Green and Gielgud scintillated as Lady Freelove and Lord Trinket. It was *The Jealous Wife* by George Colman. John wanted to play one of their scenes in a window overlooking the street. My eye fell on a large settle which we were to use in another scene. I had it placed with its back to the footlights so that one had a vista of the room within. A couple of stools on the settle seat and there we had our window in the rough. That is an example of the kind of compromise in setting that we were used to in those days. Well, it was an economy in money, in time of setting, and in stage room.

When we revived *Richard II* Richardson lifted the whole play to Gielgud's level as Bolingbroke. I took over John of Gaunt. He is one of those characters that suffer from having a speech of great beauty that is too well known.

A MAKE-UP FOR CALIBAN
Sketch by Sir Ralph Richardson.

VIII

Sadler's Wells Renascent

AND suddenly Sadler's Wells was upon us.

Lilian Baylis organized a semi-official visit of the whole company. As I stood in the vast, empty auditorium ringing with the workmen's hammers I realized that the opening, which I had secretly hoped to escape, was imminent. But I am glad to say that from that moment my enthusiasm flared up. I suggested to Lilian Baylis that we should open the theatre with a performance of *Twelfth Night* on Twelfth Night itself, January 6, and the plan was adopted. But before that there was much to be done—in fact, *Antony and Cleopatra*.

The editors have arranged for forty-two scenes in this play. I decided to abandon realism and, hanging on the coat-tails of Harley Granville-Barker and William Poel, and, with the help of Paul Smyth, we achieved a rapid sequence of events almost kaleidoscopic in effect. For costumes we went to the pictures of Paul Veronese and Tiepolo. Gielgud may not have been an ideal Antony but, as ever, he was vibrant, colourful and romantic. Dorothy Green had already won honours as Cleopatra at Stratford-on-Avon. Maurice Jacobson did the music for me and the whole company clashed together with the rhythm of the sistrums proper to the worship of Isis.

After the dress rehearsal on Friday we all realized that we were not ready. Lilian Baylis generously waived her strict rule against Sunday work and we organized a full dress rehearsal with a skeleton staff. For once we were free of the usual bogey—the race against the clock and the evening performance. Lilian Baylis came and sat in her box with us when she was not in church, which was a typical gesture on her part. I was acting the short part of the Messenger who brings the news of Antony's marriage in Rome. John sat in front for this scene and made me toe the line. Our manager told me how much she liked to see us working in that way, taking and giving criticism. But then we always did.

AQUATIC THEATRE, SADLERS WELLS.

Mᵣ C. DIBDIN'S, NIGHT.

Monday, September 22ⁿᵈ 1817.

SADLER'S WELLS THEATRE
View on a box ticket for Monday night, September 22, 1817.

The play ran for four weeks instead of the usual three, to record business. Granville-Barker came to see it and I had a talk with him about it. He objected to my having my actors 'discovered' in some scenes. I argued that I wanted to save time. He retorted that no actor can start a scene until the curtain is well up and by that time he can have entered. Of course he was right. The long entrances possible in the Elizabethan theatre are constantly used by Shakespeare, and to cut them, as we often have to on the 'picture frame' stage, damages the scene. He had other criticisms but he was not a niggard of his praise. He thought we were doing well.

Also I had a letter from Gordon Craig. He thought *Antony and Cleopatra* the best he had seen me do . . . 'All of a piece—not clever —good'. I was proud to win his praise, especially as I knew he could damn as well. He had not liked *The Tempest* at all.

A few nights before the opening there was a house-warming party given at Sadler's Wells, and it certainly needed warming. Jean Sterling

NINETTE DE VALOIS
Founder in 1931 of the Sadler's Wells Ballet.

Mackinlay sang and found it easy to sing in, but for speaking it was not good. It may be better now that a few years' dirt has collected on that hard non-resonant ferro-concrete. It was some weeks, too, before the ventilating plant was running correctly. At first it set up a low, reverberating hum which, without their knowing why, confused the ears of the audiences.

On Tuesday, January 6, 1931, the rebuilt Sadler's Wells Theatre was formally declared open by Sir Johnston Forbes-Robertson, supported by Dame Madge Kendal, Sir Reginald Rowe and others. A moment later the curtain rang up on Shakespeare's *Twelfth Night*.

It was then that my real difficulties began. It had not been realized that the public for the new theatre would have to be built up, just as had happened at the Old Vic. In the endeavour to do this there were

ALICIA MARKOVA AND ANTON DOLIN

In *Giselle*, 1933-4. These famous dancers led the ballet company during its early years, and helped to establish it. They returned as guest stars of the 1947-8 season at Covent Garden.

so many changes of policy during the next two or three years that the playgoer never knew where we were playing. Even the *habitués* of the parent theatre became confused.

Bernard Shaw came to read *Arms and the Man* to the company. He read his plays superbly. On that occasion someone kept us waiting and he entertained us with yarns about Barry Sullivan and *The Lady of Lyons*. I think it was from that play that he lifted some stage business and used it in his own way in *Arms and the Man*. His genuine love of the theatre is very plain and he exercises a great deal of charm among the players. Was it not St John Ervine who once wrote of him, ' No wonder he does not need alcohol, when he can intoxicate himself with his own wit ' ?

G.B.S. turned up at the dress rehearsal. That was not such a happy occurrence. We had got the window in the wrong place. Getting it

'SYMPHONIC VARIATIONS'
Frederick Ashton's ballet to music by César Franck had its first presentation during the 1945-6 season. Michael Somes with (left to right), Moira Shearer, Margot Fonteyn and Pamela May.

right took time. The changes of position upset the actors. Shaw borrowed my torch and used up the battery. He groaned and growled, and after the first act dressed us all down, seized an umbrella from the dark circle and dashed away to a wedding !

I could scarcely have asked for more fortunate casting than Ralph Richardson as Bluntschli and John Gielgud as Sergius.

Much Ado About Nothing—the next play—lives or dies in the Beatrice. There is no gainsaying that there is nothing in the part that Dorothy Green could not twist round her little finger, and she and Gielgud were now playing together superbly. I think I must have seen Fred Terry as Don Pedro, but, with my admiration for the Terry family, I cannot believe that he was better than Ralph Richardson.

I must break off the story of the drama because on May 5, 1931, something occurred which was to have a lasting influence on the history

'DOUANES', 1932-3

Anton Dolin, Anthony Tudor, and Ninette de Valois in the latter's ballet to music by Geoffrey Toye.

of the Old Vic. Evelyn Williams tells how in 1928 a slight figure in a gay summer frock and a huge floppy hat had an appointment with Lilian Baylis. 'She looked the ballerina she was, no more ; but when she left the office half an hour later Lilian could say with conviction : " Ninette de Valois is going to form a ballet company for us. When we open at the Wells, it will be on a whole-time basis." ' Could one have a better example of Lilian Baylis's uncanny insight into character than the decision she took in those thirty minutes ?

On that summer evening in May the Sadler's Wells Ballet was born. In a decade it was to come to ripe maturity. Truly a miraculous birth ! I was present at the accouchement.

Miss de Valois tells me that it was a hectic evening. The dancers came from all over London—Anton Dolin hurried over in a car from the Hippodrome, for instance—and times had to be fitted to a split second, just like one of those Birthday nights. The house was packed and Dolin brought it down with a Spanish dance which, I think, he had to encore twice. Among others in the programme were Lydia Lopokova, Hedley Briggs, Stanley Judson, Ursula Moreton, Sheila

'LE LAC DES CYGNES', 1934-5

Alicia Markova and the Sadler's Wells corps de ballet with Robert Helpmann, who
joined the company in 1932.

McCarthy, Joy Newton and Leslie French. The conductor was
Constant Lambert, who thus began his long association with the ballet.
This night proved so successful that two more were given at the newly
opened Wells.

It was two years before the ballet had a chance to make any real
headway. The Camargo Society and Phyllis Bedells helped, the first by
allowing the ballet to use some of the Society's productions and the latter
by dancing at the Wells. Then *Job* was produced, the first financial
success and the English Ballet's only subsidy. In the spring of 1932
Anton Dolin and Markova were engaged as principal dancers.
Audiences rapidly increased in numbers and the Governors (led no
doubt by Lilian Baylis) put the ballet on the same footing as the drama
and opera.

Ninette de Valois had already founded her school, but in the beginning
the *corps de ballet* consisted of six young women. By 1937 it comprised
twenty women and twelve men, two resident choreographers, a resident
conductor, and a school of forty students employing a full-time staff;
and about ninety per cent of the 1938 company graduated from it.

'HAMLET'

Robert Helpmann's notable ballet to music by Tchaikovsky was first produced in 1942, with décor by Leslie Hurry. Left to right : John Hunt (Laertes), Gordon Hamilton (Polonius), David Paltenghi (King), Robert Helpmann (Hamlet). Extreme right : Celia Franca (Queen).

Some time in 1932 a young man arrived from Australia. He called on Ninette de Valois with a letter of introduction. To use Robert Helpmann's own words : ' She came in, and the restful, lazy days of my life went out ! She looked at me, " You know, something could be done with that face." ' Before long he was sharing the leads with Harold Turner. His future is well known to all of us. Other dancers pirouette and take their bow—Margot Fonteyn, Pamela May, Michael Somes, Ninette de Valois herself, and many more.

The list of designers increased to a score ; and the home team of choreographers—including Frederick Ashton, Robert Helpmann and Ninette de Valois—was reinforced by distinguished artists from abroad. Serguëeff from the Imperial Ballet in St Petersburg came as *maître de ballet*, thus making a direct link with the classical tradition.

Tours in Britain were undertaken with success and the ballet was honoured by being chosen to represent that branch of the British Theatre during the International Exhibition in Paris in May 1937.

And then the war came. The ballet continued to give performances —their record was forty-eight weeks out of fifty-two. In the May of

1940 they began a tour of Holland, Belgium, and France, under the British Council. All things considered, it was a brave and courageous enterprise. They were nearly trapped when the German advance began that ended in the fall of France. The scenery, costumes and scores of some eight ballets had to be abandoned, though I believe a little has now been recovered. The company lost their personal belongings other than what they could take in a handbag, with the exception of some stalwarts, who dressed themselves in three suits of clothes ! They played at Sadler's Wells that summer (and the opera too) and then, when the raids started and all London theatres closed down, went on tour. They would now have had no London home had not Bronson Albery thrown open the doors of the New Theatre, where they gave a season with two pianos instead of an orchestra. It proved so successful that they returned for crowded seasons until just before the end of hostilities. On behalf of the Governors, Bronson Albery now took over the management of the ballet with his son, Donald Albery, as business manager. Ninette de Valois looks upon Bronson Albery as the saviour of the Sadler's Wells Ballet and she of all people should know.

In 1945 the company toured the Continent under E.N.S.A. and the British Council for two months, and in 1946 an arrangement was made with the Covent Garden Opera Trust whereby the ballet appeared at the Royal Opera House, Covent Garden.

At the present time there is not only the ballet working at Covent Garden, but also an auxiliary company at Sadler's Wells Theatre. The two theatres now have some eighty dancers, and the parent company is able to draw recruits from the Wells as it needs them. And the Wells draws on the school now firmly established in Colet Gardens. There students get a full education as well as their training for the ballet. All this magnificent work has grown out of the industry and inspiration of one woman, backed, originally, by another so utterly different in temperament, and yet both aiming at a common target. Even those who hold but a poor opinion of Lilian Baylis will admit that she was a good chooser when looking for craftsmanship. In that half-hour interview Evelyn Williams writes of, Lilian must have seen more than a floppy hat.

In 1947 Ninette de Valois was made a C.B.E. We rejoiced that she should be so honoured for her own sake and for the prestige of the Sadler's Wells Ballet, but I think that she has a richer reward that is renewed in her heart every working day of her life.

The last play of the season was to be *King Lear* instead of the usual revival of *Hamlet*. Edith Evans had given us a couple of great pillars from some production of hers. I used them in *Antony and Cleopatra* and again now, and also some intriguing rostrums designed for the Caldecott Community. We managed some pretty good rugged effects with these in combination. If we judge by box-office standards, the production was an overwhelming success. It even filled the Wells— which was no easy task in those days. *King Lear* is the hardest, the most difficult nut to crack of the whole gamut of plays and it was cheering to hear from Gordon Bottomley that, in his opinion, we had touched a high-water mark. Now I come to think of it the majority of my letters— other than those of the disgruntled last-ditchers—were from poets.

For Gloucester's two sons we welcomed two guests in Robert Speaight as Edmund and Eric Portman as Edgar.

Because of the rites and ceremonies of the last night *King Lear* was too long, so we gave *Much Ado About Nothing* instead. It was a sad night for me for I was losing Dorothy Green, Leslie French, and John Gielgud. John's going was to rob me not only of an actor of the highest ability and, without overstatement, one who at times should be termed great, but also of a dear comrade who always held his position in the company with absolute fairness and consideration for his fellow artists. His

CONSTANT LAMBERT
Musical director and conductor of the Sadler's Wells Ballet from 1931 to 1947.

departure had but a material finality. His charm (that Terry quality he secretly fears !), his craftsmanship, his influence are still there.

My happiness lay in the fact that I had persuaded Ralph Richardson to come back at the head of the company. I wonder how many miles I trod in the quiet streets behind the Friends' Meeting House off the Euston Road before I wrung acceptance from him ? His mood was diffident, I might almost say obstinate, and he was doubtful of his ability to play such a wide range of parts. He could not believe in the rich humour of his Sir Toby Belch, the virility of his Kent, and the lyric beauty and tragic feeling of his Enobarbus.

RALPH RICHARDSON AND EDITH EVANS
As Iago and Emilia in *Othello*, 1931-2.

IX

The Working-day World

G. K. CHESTERTON, in a broadcast talk, once drew attention to some of the common miracles of life, which, happening as they do every day, escape our notice. We go to bed, for instance, pass into a state of unconsciousness comparable to death, and are reborn every morning without the process seeming in any way significant.

Rehearsals in a repertory theatre are also unremarkable because they happen every day—'Fridays and Saturdays and all'. But the work that really builds the edifice largely depends on what happens between ten-thirty in the morning and three o'clock in the afternoon ; and that in a sense is miraculous.

It is no easy matter to get actors to the theatre by half-past ten in the morning when they are acting nightly and are habitually not in bed until close on midnight.

For myself, I like getting up early, and indeed it was a necessity if I was to attend to my own private life, deal with correspondence, and reach the theatre in time to get a word with Miss Williams about future arrangements or some immediate difficulty.

Why am I so attracted by an empty theatre in the early morning ? Does it go back to that old secret desire to know all about the working of a theatre long before I had any idea that I should one day go on the stage ? As a spectator I have always been strongly held by the illusion that a play creates, and my experience as an actor has not shaken it in any degree. I am what may be termed a good audience, and do not really enjoy going round to see players after the performance, especially when I have been at all moved. I believe this very delight in the theatre makes me an indifferent critic.

But all those who love their work have an affection for the workshop and the theatre at its best is a fine workshop.

There is a calm austerity about an empty theatre—the stage swept

'THE TAMING OF THE SHREW', 1931-2
Centre : Ralph Richardson (Petruchio) and Phyllis Thomas (Katharine) ; seated :
Leslie French (Grumio).

and bare, last night's scenery stacked in orderly packs in the wings, and the vast auditorium, shrouded in dust-sheets, but half discernible, except where a beam of light, straying from some small, unscreened window right up at the back of the gallery, shoots aslant to pick up a scroll of battered gilt on the proscenium.

And then the silence. Not a mouse stirring. It is as real a thing as is the hush that hangs in a cathedral. In its utter contrast to the turmoil of the night, it holds the mind in humility and consecration.

Viewed from the stalls, the stage is grey and misty, cavernous in depth. A stray face grows out of the darkness, peers vaguely at the auditorium, and silently vanishes. A stage-hand moves across on some mysterious errand. He seems more like a phantom than a living man. A voice high up in the flies calls a name, and then a door bangs. The stillness again descends, while a cat walks the complete width of the stage with possessive dignity, pausing but once to glance solemnly at the bass fiddle in the orchestra pit.

Presently the stage manager and his assistant arrive. With the help of one of the men they begin pushing small rostrums and chairs about. A stone bench is put in position, and a small table plac d by the footlights (' floats ' we call them), on which the stage managers place their prompt book and necessary impedimenta. Members of the company now begin to drift in, and, gathering into knots, discuss eagerly together—not, I

'HENRY V', 1931-2
Centre (left to right) : Ralph Richardson (Henry), Phyllis Thomas (French Princess),
Harcourt Williams (Charles VI).

expect, the news of the world, or high art, but the little things of life, and possibly a play that they have seen. A newcomer joins the group. He has read his name in the cast of the new play which has just been pinned on the notice-board. He will have a line to speak. He is a first-year student and his excitement is intense ; it is shared by his hearers according to their natures.

Finally, the producer emerges from his little office, clasping various objects which sort themselves out on the small table: the copy of the play on which he has worked, a reporter's notebook, a spectacle case, some special hand property that he has devised to help an actor, and a mug of milk.

The stage manager reports that someone is ill. This entails a hurried consultation. Who understudies the part that the invalid should be playing at night ? Is the understudy good enough, and does he or she know the words ? That question is settled, and the rehearsal light is switched on. We settle down to work . . . and then the cleaners begin their operations in the front of the house. A shattering distraction this, both for producer and actors struggling for their words. Sometimes an electrical vacuum cleaner will pop its snake-like head in to have a look at the carpets in the stalls, but its voice is so unrhythmical that it has to be ordered out. I never knew a theatre that did not suffer from such morning visitations, so I can only conclude that the cleaners are subject to some cosmic law that forbids them to function at any other time.

The rehearsal proceeds. The play is *Twelfth Night*. The lords and ladies attendant on Count Orsino are students, and have to be grouped effectively and taught how to express interest in the scene without obtruding themselves. Curio is late. His excuse is that he has been helping an old lady up the escalator. The producer deals with this social problem as his mind darts away, and sees, in a second's beat, himself cast by Mr Benson for the boy Lucius in *Julius Caesar*. His mother dashes up to Southport to see her eighteen-year-old stripling act this pleasing part ; but, alas, in the interim, Lucius has been torn away and given to a girl (a great, lubberly girl, thinks the sex-proud youth), and Mr Benson has offered Curio as a sop. Young hopeful hastens to his Shakespeare to ' study ' the part. Here it is :

CURIO : *Will you go hunt, my lord ?*
DUKE : *What, Curio ?*
CURIO : *The hart.*

And that contains it all. Southport would scarcely be impressed, however brilliantly one said the words ! But only in disappointment can we find its philosophical antidote.

In the middle of the next scene Rowley, the carpenter, arrives. An unexpected demand for a certain scene cloth has arrived from ' the opera ' at Sadler's Wells. Can he take it down ? It is a nuisance, but he can. The scene is lowered from the flies and rolled up and dispatched as discreetly as may be, but the interruption plays havoc with the rehearsal. We seize the opportunity of persuading Rowley to give us something that we need for the coming production, and when peace is at last restored ' on we go ', as Irving used to exclaim in moments of stress.

Now it is time for a break. The company retires to the canteen for twenty minutes, and the producer sits in his solitary stall regaling himself with the bread and cheese that some kind-hearted student has scivvied for him. Perhaps an actor will drift back to beguile him of some future part he wants to play, or to discuss some business of the play. Paul Smyth, clad in paint-bespattered overall, makes a harassed descent from the wardrobe to gather and make suggestions, or fling lengths of glittering material, where they may be tested for stage use, in the sudden beam of a spotlight.

For the last hour and a half or so after the break the pace is definitely slower ; signs of exhaustion appear, and a diet of buns and coffee dims the Thespian sparkle.

The last scene is tackled with its rather complicated movements.

An actor complains that the producer told him something quite different on the previous day. Probably this is true, but in production a play grows in the producer's mind as well as on the stage, and modifications of the original design become necessary. Again, if an actor is self-conscious, inflexible, by altering instructions from time to time the producer may sometimes break down the barriers : knead the clay, as it were, until it becomes malleable. It is a painful process for the actor, but out of it often emerges a performance that is unexpected in its excellence. Sometimes the producer leaps upon the stage to show how a little ' bit ' may be done. It comes off, and the younger members of the cast utter sighs of appreciation. Thus the producer (if he has had acting experience) can acquire a reputation for a brilliance which is largely fictitious. It is one thing to carry off a few lines in an effective situation, and quite another to sustain a long part !

The rehearsal is dismissed, and the players hurry homewards to get a little rest before the evening. The understudy stays behind and is put through his paces. He will do, and goes his way to the wardrobe to find garments that will fit. Maybe a piece of ' raw material ' stays behind too for a little extra polish, and then the producer gathers up his belongings and goes off to an interview with some possible future player, to deal with matters for the Press, or to have a word with Lilian Baylis.

Busier than ever now between the two theatres, she is not easy to catch. If the dogs bark as one enters the passage, she is sure to be in her office. The dogs are evicted from their favourite chair and, after the hubbub of stern commands, endearments, and yapping has subsided, the welcome is always a warm one. Maternal instincts are suspect these days, but the right thing at such a moment is not to be despised. It is really a gentle dictator that sits in that office, surrounded by pictures of her friends and those odds and ends that are so personal to her. The secret of her power is that she cares. She cares passionately for her cause, and she cares for people. Humanity might be a larger word to use, but do we not mean by that : ' You and me and all of us ' ?

Amazing woman, to have brought two such theatres into being, and not to have lost the serenity of her purpose !

The negotiations close. One may leave the office defeated, but indubitably braced.

The producer makes his way across the dark back of the circle. Down on the stage he observes two or three youngsters trying out a little acting on their own. Unseen, he watches for a while. How attractive they seem in the dim shafts of bluish light ! And he reflects what effective stage pictures come at rehearsal—pictures and impressions

'ABRAHAM LINCOLN', 1931-2
Harcourt Williams in the title role of the first Old Vic production of John
Drinkwater's play.

that an audience can never see when make-up masks the delicate movements of the face muscles, and the glaring lights disperse the mysteries.

'That girl does well,' he thinks, and, vaguely considering her in some future cast, he wanders out into the twilight of Waterloo Road.

An interval, and then back again to see how the present play is growing in performance, to correct an item of 'business' here, to re-time the fall of a curtain there, to hurry up a change of scene and, on this night, to see how the understudy gets on.

Home again, where the routine of life is smooth enough to pass unnoticed (but that means responsibility for someone !)—and so to bed, with the Folio propped on knees, planning some play that will not become an urgent matter for a month or more. A rare half-hour of creative pleasure, untrammelled, fancy-free ; until he that knits up the ravelled sleeve of care enfolds us in that Chestertonian oblivion which each tomorrow makes a womb of miracle, fruitful in vigorous new birth.

X

Plummet Sound

A FEW days before we assembled for rehearsals at the beginning of my third season, there was a happening of momentous importance to this country and the world. Britain went off the gold standard and we were plunged into the 1931 financial crisis. The world of the theatre suffered with the rest. I was so absorbed in my job that I did not realize at the time what it would mean to us. It came, too, at a most unfortunate time when we were struggling with the problems with which Sadler's Wells had faced us.

Lilian Baylis made a fighting speech at the first rehearsal. She reminded us that when the world was in trouble people came to the Old Vic for relaxation. It was one of those occasions when one saw the bright flame of her spirit. She prophesied that we should do a good season, but she did not foresee the Press campaign for economy carried to absurd lengths.

King John had some good things in it. I now think it was not a wise play with which to open. It should have come later in the season when the company was working together. I had one or two weak spots in the casting, but towers of strength in Robert Harris, Robert Speaight and Ralph Richardson.

We dealt with the difficult battle scenes in an unrealistic manner. Farquharson Small helped me here, and so did Herbert Menges with a stirring drum composition. The battle scenes only present difficulties to a modern, film-saturated audience. The Globe ' groundlings ' were obviously satisfied with a token army.

Farquharson Small, with Scottish insistence, had gate-crashed the Old Vic last season. He hurled sketches at me, he stood on my private doorstep, he threatened suicide. Finally he married ' Arthur ' in the person of Pat Maloney. He and Paul Smyth worked together on *The Taming of the Shrew*. I modelled the production on the *Commedia del Arte* to the music of Scarlatti, and made use of the Christopher Sly scenes from an old play, *A Taming of a Shrew.*

Then followed a repercussion from the financial crisis. Sir Reginald Rowe took such a serious view of the situation that he did not think we could survive the year unless we could effect some improvement. This meant a change in the bill every three weeks instead of every four, and now that we were playing every night and two matinees, plus L.C.C. school matinees, it meant that the time for production was very short indeed. The players were over-worked, they had no time to learn their lines, and illness increased which meant more loss of time spent in getting understudies on. My energy and patience began to wear thin and the standard of work began to slip. To soften the blow at first, I was able to put on *A Midsummer Night's Dream.* The chief innovation here was a mask I invented for the Ass's head. It had the great advantage of allowing Richardson to use his own eyes.

Henry V turned the tide. Robert Speaight did his best work in a first-rate performance of Fluellen, and Phyllis Thomas was very happy as the French Princess. I was her father, Charles VI. The whole company flamed together. Well, you see it was November and this was our fourth production. That is the sovereign value of a repertory company. Ralph Richardson's Henry was remarkable. He was not the Henry that the hero-worshippers wanted. He put a certain hard, almost cruel quality into it. He was a statesman and a general, but with a human touch beneath the glitter of kingship. One can always be certain that his emotion will ring true.

On the opening night of our next play, *The Knight of the Burning Pestle*, a woman climbed out of the orchestra pit—the pit of an Elizabethan playhouse for the nonce—and exclaimed : ' By your leave, gentlemen, I'm a stranger here. I was ne'er at one of these plays before ! ' A burst of laughter greeted this statement which was followed by a boisterous welcome from the house ; for it was spoken by their old favourite Sybil Thorndike in the part of the Citizen's Wife. Richardson was, of course, the Ralph, a part with which he romped away with the resourcefulness of a music-hall comedian right up to the moment when he ascended heavenwards like an inebriated Ganymede.

The Sadler's Wells audiences were now clamouring to be spoon-fed. They wanted the story of the play printed in the programme. That meant a new job for the producer. But I refused to give away the *dénouement.* If they could not understand that I did not much care.

An all-star cast of *Julius Caesar* was announced at His Majesty's Theatre just before we started our production. Result ? The Lower Marsh lovers of Shakespeare waited for the heavenly galaxy in the

'MACBETH', 1932-3

Malcolm Keen played the title role in this production, with Margaret Webster as Lady Macbeth.

Haymarket. Astronomically speaking, the light from some of the stars had been travelling a considerable number of years.

Richardson's Brutus was better than most I have seen. He was the soldier, the philosopher, the idealist. But he missed that metaphysical something in the character that Shakespeare was to develop more fully in Hamlet. Maybe it was foreign to Richardson's scientific outlook. The final scene leading to his self-destruction was clear-cut and magnificent.

I now had the advantage of two staircases from the orchestra pit (I used it as part of the Forum) which made the handling of the crowds much easier. Those staircases are no more but they have their counterpart in stone at the Wells. My memorial!

Lilian Baylis had a great liking for John Drinkwater's play *Abraham Lincoln*. I was to play the leading part and the author was to produce. Everything was going swimmingly until Drinkwater became seriously ill, and I had to shoulder the production as well as the long part of Lincoln. The play fitted our company very happily. Phyllis Thomas was as good as the original Susan Deddington (Cathleen Orford).

'CAESAR AND CLEOPATRA', 1932-3
The leading parts in this production of Shaw's play were taken by Peggy Ashcroft
and Malcolm Keen (seated, centre).

Douglas Jefferies as Seward, and Richardson as General Grant both
scored. I went to endless trouble about my appearance but made one
serious blunder. I wore my own hair, which is most unlike Lincoln's
in shape and colour.

I had a great disappointment in the next revival. It was *Othello* and
Ralph promised to be an exceptional Iago. He had the glamour of
good fellowship and ingenuous honesty which I have only seen realized
since in Anthony Quayle's performance in 1947. But by the time we
opened Richardson was having trouble with his voice, and one afternoon
he was in such pain that it was clear he could not finish the matinee.
He has since told me that with wild, determined eyes I tore the clothes
from him and with book in hand rushed down the stairs to finish the
part. Fortunately I was able to get Alastair Sim to take it on afterwards.
Edith Evans as Emilia returned to the scene of her triumphs, and
Wilfrid Walter was Othello.

When the play was produced about 1600 the event of the Turkish
attack on Cyprus was only some thirty years old, so I aimed at getting
that topical touch into the playing. Instead of the senators sitting robed

'THE ADMIRABLE BASHVILLE', 1932-3
The final tableau of Shaw's 'burlesque'. Leading parts were played by Roger
Livesey and Valerie Tudor.

and bechained in their places I had them rushing in—just roused from
their beds and finishing their dressing as they came.

A few weeks before the opening of Sadler's Wells Lilian Baylis had
to have an operation. She carried on as best she could from the hospital
near by with dogged determination. One pretended that it was fun
talking over details of the work with her in a kind of tent which screened
off her bed from the ward, but it made the heart ache to see her lying
there just when her deeply desired scheme was coming to fruition.
She took up normal working life too soon, which, coupled with the
excitement of opening the new theatre, brought on a slight relapse.
One day she drove me from one theatre to the other and talked about
the future. She wanted me to stay for one more season. Experience
had taught her that a producer is bound to feel the strain at the end
of four years, and an audience tires of a single man's ideas no matter
how hard-working or brilliant he may be. As we turned up Rosebery
Avenue and the square red building of the Wells came into sight, she
wondered what would happen when there was no Lilian Baylis. She
spoke as though she would be glad to hand over her heavy burden now

if only she could find the right successor. Of course she would never have done this. It was her illness that made her yearn for some kind of rest. She did begin to hand over the reins to Tyrone Guthrie and others later, but it was to be half a dozen years before she found her real rest. I don't think I ever got nearer to the real Lilian than I did on that drive, nor was I ever so conscious of her dearness.

Edith Evans stayed to play Viola in *Twelfth Night*. Somewhere Granville-Barker has written, ' To tell a woman to begin her study of how to play a woman's part by imagining herself a boy may seem absurd ; but this is the right approach nevertheless.' He is speaking of Shakespeare's women, of course, and I am convinced that Edith Evans approached Viola from that point of view. Every syllable of the soliloquy after Malvolio has left her with the ring was sheer delight.

I now had to pay the penalty for what I can only describe as a piece of wild folly on my part. In order to persuade the two Roberts—Messrs Speaight and Harris—to come for this season I had promised the part of Hamlet to both of them. At the time the financial crisis had not shortened our time for production from four to three weeks. However, we did it—' Entireties ' and all.

It was interesting to watch these two Hamlets because in their excellence they were so different—two sides of the medal as it were. Robert Harris's characterization had all the indecision, the infirmity of purpose, and the poetic idealism that made him unable to deal with examples gross as earth, whereas in Speaight the vigorous activity that made him rush to the battlements, and burn with enthusiasm over the play that was to be the mousetrap to catch a king, were stronger than the pale cast of thought that held his revenge in check. One felt that could these two Hamlets have been one person, the King would have been slain ten minutes after the Ghost had said ' Remember me ! '

So season number three came to an end and in Ralph Richardson I lost an actor of the highest quality and a friend into the bargain—which reminds me that Gielgud came to two of our plays during that season and wrote me long letters packed with splendid criticism and not a little praise which I hugged to my heart.

That summer I walked and talked with George Bernard Shaw on the Malvern Hills. We were supposed to be debating the opening play of next season, *Caesar and Cleopatra*. But beyond describing to me a picture he had seen of a camp fire sending up a long, thin column of smoke in the still air of the desert which, I think he said, had given him the idea of the first scene, and telling me a story about Sir Johnston Forbes-Robertson in the part of Caesar, we did not approach the subject !

Forbes-Robertson's performance was by far the best I have seen.

'THE MERCHANT OF VENICE', 1932-3

A suitor at Belmont. Portia (Peggy Ashcroft) greets the Prince of Morocco
(Anthony Quayle).

His final exit up on to the ship with a great purple sail rising behind him was a thing of beauty. Malcolm Keen, who had joined us enthusiastically as leading man, started well with Caesar, and Peggy Ashcroft was ideal as Cleopatra.

Shaw came to see the production and sent me a crowded postcard of helpful notes. One has a sad historical interest—'When they jump into the water you should have *buckets of rice* thrown up to shew the splash'. He seems to have liked the production. But, alas, we were soon to have our first blow. Peggy Ashcroft broke her toe and had to retire from the play and also miss some of the rehearsals for *Cymbeline*. I put this play into the fifteenth century and gave Imogen a loom in her scenes with Iachimo, after Pinturicchio's picture of ' The Return of Ulysses ', and I had a eurhythmic battle arranged by Winifred Houghton.

Sickert did a sketch of Peggy Ashcroft as Rosalind in the act of putting the chain round Orlando's neck. I don't wonder that he wanted to paint her. Malcolm Keen was at his best, I think, in parts that called for leisured humour, and Jaques, and Old Hardcastle in *She Stoops to Conquer*, were both admirably done.

But before that Edward Carrick (Gordon Craig's son) came to do

PEGGY ASHCROFT AS ROSALIND
In *As You Like It*, 1932-3.

Macbeth. I say ' do ' because he designed the scenery, costumes and properties ; many of the last he made himself, and would arrive in a derelict car sprouting with magnificent spears. He is such a well-trained man of the theatre and an expert draughtsman. Why does the theatre allow the films to steal him away ?

Margaret Webster, now so famous in America, came to play Lady Macbeth. She shared with us the misfortunes of that tragedy. Keen slipped in the fight and hurt his back. Marius Goring who had played the part abroad took it up at a moment's notice. But he was only

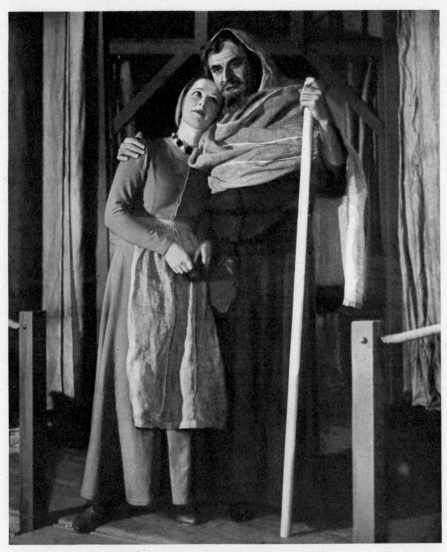

MALCOLM KEEN AND VALERIE TUDOR
In *The Merchant of Venice*, 1932-3.

about twenty at the time, so John Laurie was invited to conclude the
run. Poor Peggy Webster; Lady Macbeth became a kind of
Scheherazade. Three husbands in as many weeks!

Marius Goring, whom I had known since childhood, came to me
straight from school. I remember his reciting to me a difficult poem
of Browning's, 'Caliban upon Setebos', up in the rehearsal room. I
knew at once that the right thing was there and wanted him to join us
as a student, but for some reason Lilian Baylis did not want him. So
I smuggled him into *Julius Caesar* about 1930 when we had some students

from London University to swell the crowd, and he stayed with us and finished up by playing Romeo to Peggy Ashcroft's Juliet. Before that happened John Gielgud undertook a production of *The Merchant of Venice*. The décor was by ' Motley ' and the music from Peter Warlock's ' Capriol ' suite. The whole set was done in unpainted hessian (which lights to a rich gold), and ingeniously devised to cover the entire play. I was cast for the Prince of Aragon and was supposed to have a rest, but some film complication tore Gielgud away from us a great deal and I was left to carry out his plan as best I could.

She Stoops to Conquer followed. Clare Harris joined for Mrs Hardcastle, and she and Roger Livesey as Tony Lumpkin romped finely through the play.

Mid-season illness began to overtake us. Anthony Quayle went down at the dress rehearsal of *The Winter's Tale* and I found myself reading lines held in the palm of my hand as First Lord. What little joy I had in that production is centred on Livesey and Morland Graham as the Shepherds, and on Peggy Ashcroft as Perdita and Charles Hickman as the Steward.

Peggy was the next casualty. She was ill and almost voiceless on the first night of *Mary Stuart*. She gallantly played on and by the end of the run was giving a lovely performance. I had acted Darnley in this play of Drinkwater's at the Everyman Theatre, Hampstead, and Clare Harris had played Mary Beaton, and now we played them again.

The Admirable Bashville—Shaw's burlesque—went swimmingly from beginning to end. Roger Livesey and Valerie Tudor set the pace and we all had tremendous fun.

Romeo and Juliet, which followed, was on the whole a better production than my first, but illness still disrupted rehearsals. Marius Goring's Romeo was extraordinarily good, but at that time his voice lacked musical quality. By the time we reached *The School for Scandal* everyone was well and the whole company on their toes—in fact, an end of season ensemble. Veronica Turleigh came back to play Lady Sneerwell. It was really a very strong company that season, headed by Keen, Peggy Ashcroft, Livesey, Morland Graham, Alastair Sim, Charles Hickman, William Fox, Marius Goring, George Devine, Anthony Quayle, Geoffrey Wincott, Clare Harris, and Frank Napier. Both in this play and in the Goldsmith comedy I cut all gags and wiped away all traditional business, and put an embargo on so-called period postures and lace-handkerchief tricks. I attempted to restore the balance of the screen scene. Hickman as Charles did not attempt to score laughs at the end of it, and Peggy Ashcroft did not use the situation as an opportunity for a display of intense emotional acting.

After dashing on for Gielgud as Prospero a year or two back I was bitten by a desire to play the part in comfort. So we finished up with *The Tempest*, and Leslie French came back for Ariel.

For various reasons this last season had not been an entirely happy one, but I owed a great deal to the help and cheer that Peggy Ashcroft gave me. Her insight and clear-headedness, and her own particular technique which demands absolute honesty and freedom from any suspicion of false sentiment were invaluable. She does not know what it means to use a ' trick ' ; she has an eye for line and colour and instinctively rejects the commonplace. No wonder she made such lovely people of the parts she played.

Before the last night I had a letter from Lilian. In it she said, ' You must know that you have done good work here, and I like to hope that you will remember your " Four Years Hard " with happiness.' The dear quality of that letter speaks for itself. ' Four Years Hard ' was going to be the title of my book. From the end of it I quote :

' I am crossing the Old Vic stage. It is littered with new scenery in the making . . . Why the dickens didn't I try a demand for everything new ? I reach the office to find it agog with coming and going of messengers, telephone calls, fluttering papers. It is the morning of the first rehearsal. On such a day no one has time for visitors, and such am I now. The whole place is vibrating with anticipations of the coming season . . . I slip unobtrusively away . . .'

XI

The Laughton Invasion

WHEN I attended the opening night of the next season my sensations were extremely complicated. In those days when old favourites entered the stalls they received a startling ovation not from one part of the house alone but from the whole of it. I had forgotten about this and it took me utterly by surprise. It was inevitable that my thoughts should be full of memories and that I should hug a kind of nostalgia which that kind of greeting was bound to accentuate, but naturally I was ready to welcome and appreciate the new régime to the full.

The work that Tyrone Guthrie has done for the Old Vic in the last decade is inestimable ; but that first season of his—well, it was drastic, but, taking a long view, probably the best thing to do. It opened a kind of flood-gate. Have you noticed when travelling by train that it always seems to be the working-class dwellings that got bombed most ? We at the Vic were always a working class, and weary sometimes with struggling against odds—all of us from Lilian Baylis down to the girl who swept up the paper in the pit. Guthrie descended like a bomb. There was a crash and a great sheet of flame—Laughton, Robson, Seyler, Livesey, Jeans, new scenery, new costumes, all blazing to the stars ! And then, when the smoke blew away . . . much rubbish had vanished and in the open space something new began to take shape. Many *habitués* of the audience took exception to the change. We were told that the atmosphere of the place had been violated. But then, if they will forgive my reminding them, this was not the first time that they had protested. Change always disturbs the human, but he cannot do without it. I have said this before and I shall probably say it again.

Twelfth Night was the opening play. It was played in a set modelled on the Elizabethan plan and designed by Wells-Coates, the architect. Unfortunately it could be used in only two other plays because of its weight. I am not sure that it is wise to bring experts into the theatre from

TYRONE GUTHRIE
Producer at the Old Vic, 1933-4 and 1936-9 ; and with the Old Vic company at the
New Theatre, 1944-5 and 1946-7. Administrator of the Old Vic and Sadler's Wells theatres
1939-45.

'TWELFTH NIGHT', 1933-4

The opening production of Guthrie's first season. Lydia Lopokova (second from left) appeared as Olivia, and Ursula Jeans (third from left) as Viola. A young actor (on the right) made an appearance in a small part : James Mason as Valentine.

other spheres. The stage seems so simple from the auditorium, but it has one or two laws about which it is essential to know something.

Leon Quartermaine was the Malvolio, and Lydia Lopokova the Olivia. There is something so childlike and unusual about her personality that she should have been good. But I could not persuade myself that she was. Maybe her rather deliberate English with its foreign accent, piquant enough in itself, was too great a handicap. How her dancing always delighted ! I once had the good fortune—when the B.B.C. did Stravinsky's *Tale of a Soldier*—to sit alone on the stage of the Arts Theatre and watch her dance. I noticed a newcomer, James Mason by name, in the small part of Valentine. It was a gay production. Roger Livesey, Ursula Jeans, and Athene Seyler gave promise of the brilliant season before us.

The production of *The Cherry Orchard* which followed was one of the

'The Cherry Orchard', 1933-4

Charles Laughton came to the Old Vic from Hollywood for this season, and made his
debut in a presentation by Guthrie of Chekhov's play. Left to right : Leon Quartermaine
(Gaev), Athene Seyler (Madame Ranevsky), Charles Laughton (Lopahin).

Vic's peak successes. It ranked with the Russell Thorndike *Peer Gynt* in
drawing power, and it presented Chekhov's masterpiece as a gay,
vigorous comedy swept clean of the tiresome, pretentious unreality that for
so long smothered Ibsen's plays in this country. The greatest credit is
due to Tyrone Guthrie for handling this revival in such a new way.

Charles Laughton was not able to get back from Hollywood until this
production. On the first night in the part of Lopahin I felt that he had
just stepped off the boat and had not yet got his bearings in the Waterloo
Road. Athene Seyler is too good an actress not to give a first-rate
performance in whatever part she plays, and as Madame Ranevsky she
made a success ; but it was not an ideal performance of the part. Maybe
it is outside the scope of our temperament. I was in the original
production of *The Cherry Orchard* in England when the Stage Society did
it in 1911. I fear we made a poor job of it. Many of the cast thought it

'HENRY VIII', 1933-4

The 'Trial' scene: centre, Flora Robson (Queen Katharine); left, Charles
Laughton (Henry); right, Robert Farquharson (Wolsey).

was midsummer madness and the intellectuals in front were not much
wiser. I was the Student Trofimov, and I watched Dennis Arundell's
clever performance at the Old Vic with an appreciation. The first
night was an exciting evening and the public rose to the production not
only then, but throughout the run.

Laughton had just made a startling success in the Korda film *The
Private Life of Henry VIII*, and it was a mistake, I think, to choose to appear
in Shakespeare's play which does not supply an actor with a very good
part. I don't remember it as one of Guthrie's happiest productions.
Perhaps the shadow of the over-flamboyant film fell too heavily across
it. Robert Farquharson as Cardinal Wolsey made his only appearance
at the Old Vic. Remembering his admirable work in *The Cenci*, as the
crazy Duke in *The Duchess of Malfi*, and particularly as a most sensitive
Uncle Vanya, I do not think I should have cast him for that stout
statesman friend of Henry. Previously I had asked him if he would act
for me, and in that attractive halting speech which he assumes in private

'MEASURE FOR MEASURE', 1933-4
Left to right : Flora Robson (Isabella), Dennis Arundell (Lucio), Ernest Hare (Provost), Charles Laughton (Angelo).

life he replied, ' C-come to the Old Vic w-where they play things c-called *The Dream* and *The Merchant* ? No thank you ! ' It may be that he was not happy there, and retired into his shell. More than once he seemed placed at a disadvantage when possibly he might have insisted on the Cardinal's prestige to obtain a better one. Flora Robson was the Katharine, which seemed to suit her own particular quality. It was a fine picture of a woman fighting against legal conventions and an inexorable Church.

By the time *Measure for Measure* was reached, the company had learned to work together and a very fine performance was the result which drew the town—to the amazement of the management who had always listed this play with the unpopular ones. The Duke can be rather a dull part in careless hands, but Roger Livesey treated him with great skill, and the natural integrity which comes through all his acting was extremely valuable in this part. In the last scene, when Lucio suddenly tore the friar's robe from him and discovered him in his golden

'LOVE FOR LOVE', 1933-4
Left to right : Barrie Livesey (Valentine Legend), Dennis Arundell (Scandal),
Athene Seyler (Mrs Frail), Charles Laughton (Tattle).

dress, the effect was electric and, one might affirm, symbolic of his rich performance.

Charles Laughton's Angelo was, I think, the finest thing he did in that season. His scenes with Flora Robson as Isabella were admirably composed and carried out. The sinister streak often noticeable in his acting could not have been used to better advantage.

Before Miss Robson had become so well known, it was suggested to me that she would make a good leading lady at the Old Vic. I can never forgive myself for letting that chance go by.

The Tempest I saw from the gallery. Elsa Lanchester gave a highly stylized interpretation of Ariel. The pitfall awaiting those who indulge in that particular form of art is that the spectator too often is set thinking about the style instead of about the character and its relation to the play.

Oscar Wilde made the acquaintance of the Lower Marsh and the Islington heights with his *Importance of Being Earnest* and won complete

'THE TEMPEST', 1933-4

Left to right : Elsa Lanchester (Ariel), Charles Laughton (Prospero), Dennis Arundell (Antonio), Ernest Hare (Sebastian).

success, I understand. The Annual Report tells me that 'Charles Laughton again disdained the obvious and contented himself with the small part of Canon Chasuble.' I hope the wording was inspired by some personal admiration and that the man from Hollywood was not really permitted to direct the management in the matter of casting !

Congreve's *Love for Love* was given only at Sadler's Wells, in settings by Vivian Forbes, and the last play of the season was *Macbeth*. The permanent set was used for this and the costumes were designed by John Armstrong. Flora Robson had her best opportunity in Lady Macbeth and took it magnificently. Her comrade in crime was cast in less heroic mould. He was more of the Sassenach tradesman than the Highland laird. In the final battle scenes Guthrie brought off one of his brilliant effects by bringing hosts of men armed with tall spears flooding over the built-up sides of his set. It was a thrilling sight.

These last pages may seem lacking in warmth and appreciation. That is not my intention. The season was indeed a brilliant one and served many good purposes. It broke down that nagging cheese-paring business over production expenses and it struck a blow at the fetish of the Green Leaflet. Perhaps I am a shade too conscious that Laughton was not entirely happy in the Waterloo Road. Indeed, from what he once said to me I gathered that he had no great liking for Lilian Baylis. One cannot blame him for that. People of her calibre inspire dislike and love equally, but it is unusual for anyone who has played a season of leading parts not to have discovered a shade of greatness in her.

There can be no doubt that the ultimate value of this Guthrie-Laughton season to the Old Vic was remarkable. As I have already suggested it shook the traditions and outlook of the theatre to its foundations. It brought down the hard light of the Press upon it and flooded the stalls with the Smart Set from the West End theatres. More money was spent on the productions, higher salaries were paid to the players than ever before, and it was during this season that both theatres won exemption from the Entertainment Tax—the first theatres, I believe, to be granted this concession. We had some exciting productions and moments of fine acting. All this was to the good.

What was lost sight of was the worth of a repertory company—of the advantages to be gained from a group of artists not overshadowed by one or two personalities, but working together to the end that a perfect ensemble might be achieved. Lilian Baylis always had a prejudice against what she called 'West-Endy people', and fundamentally she was right. Her vision of the theatre was of the earth. She did not think of it as art with a capital A, but as solid work and a gift to her public, which her Almighty might look upon and see that it was good.

We now know that this ecstatic season did not become a precedent. It passed away leaving behind it only its trail of glory and its good, and when Tyrone Guthrie returned later he reaped the benefit of it.

XII

Henry Cass

BETWEEN the wars a little theatre was built adjoining a fine Georgian
house near the centre of Croydon and run as a repertory theatre. A
young man, Henry Cass by name, was the producer there for two or
three years and scored some successes, one or two of which were transferred to the West End. He was the next Old Vic producer to be
appointed after Tyrone Guthrie's empyreal year when certain stars shot
madly from their spheres.

Antony and Cleopatra rang up the curtain on Cass's direction. To open
a season with a new company in such a difficult play displayed great
courage if not a little rashness. He was unfortunate in having an actor
playing an important part whose diction was at fault to the point of
inaudibility even in the stalls.

Early in the season a new star began to emerge in the person of
Maurice Evans. He had of course done good work before, notably in
Journey's End, and also as Edward Voysey in the revival of *The Voysey
Inheritance* at Sadler's Wells and the Shaftesbury Theatre in aid of the
Sadler's Wells Fund in 1934. However, it needs the kind of publicity
that an Old Vic audience can give for a name to attain ' drawing power '.
The public would probably be surprised to know how very few names
have that power, and even the most advertised name—film star, or
what you will—cannot save a play that the public does not like.

Maurice Evans as Richard II gave a lively, intelligent performance.
Though entirely different from Gielgud's conception it had its own
attractive qualities. In the Euripidean tragedy of *Hippolytus* his passionate
driving power carried a not very brilliant production to success. By
this time he was beginning to use too much voice. The acoustics of
the old theatre were excellent and, although the part demanded a vigorous
delivery of the verse, there was no necessity to put enough power behind
one's vocal chords to be heard in Olympia.

'THE THREE SISTERS', 1935-6
Marie Ney, Vivienne Bennett and Nancy Hornsby in Henry Cass's
production of Chekhov's play.

Judging from general report and what I myself saw, Cass was happier in his non-Shakespearean productions. *St Joan* had a five weeks' run with Felix Aylmer, Bruce Winston and Philip Leaver as guest artists. Later in the season *Major Barbara* was produced with a like satisfactory result. The author attended most of the rehearsals of both these plays, and from my own experience I can affirm that there is no author who can be more helpful or knowledgeable about our theatre craft. Shaw's way of dealing with his actors, too, was helpful without betraying the integrity of his judgement. Any sign of complacency in an actor would find a drop of lemon juice wrapped up in a questionable compliment. But if he was genuinely satisfied he would indulge in native extravagance, as after the reading of *St Joan* when the Cassons first produced it, he said to Ernest Thesiger, who had read the Dauphin, 'You can go home to bed until the dress rehearsal'!

What an example of the whirligig of time! Fifty years ago Shaw's

MARY NEWCOMB AND MAURICE EVANS
As Beatrice and Benedick in *Much Ado About Nothing*, 1934-5. Producer:
Henry Cass.

plays were put on for odd performances with makeshift casts and attracted
the attention merely of a handful of intellectuals. Now (in 1937) the
Old Vic, the self-styled home of Shakespeare, puts on a Shaw play
knowing that it will draw big houses and be a safer card to play than the
' Swan of Avon ' himself !

Sierra's *The Two Shepherds*, translated from the Spanish by Harley
and Helen Granville-Barker, was given before *Hippolytus*, and very
delightful it was, especially Morland Graham's handling of the old Curé.
The producer of this play was a young man called Michael MacOwan
who was very soon to distinguish himself in other fields.

I am told that, in the opinion of many, Mary Newcomb's Beatrice
in *Much Ado About Nothing* was a performance of great beauty and the
best thing she did at the Old Vic.

Guest artists became the fashion in this and the next year's season—
Cathleen Nesbitt for Katharina in *The Taming of the Shrew*, George

ION SWINLEY AND WILLIAM DEVLIN
As Von Eberkopf (a part Swinley doubled with that of the Button Moulder) and
Peer in Cass's revival of *Peer Gynt* during the 1935-6 season. The play was newly
translated by R. Ellis Roberts. The settings were by Eric Newton.

Merritt as Falstaff in *Henry IV, Part II*, Buena Bent as Mistress Quickly,
and Marie Ney and Nancy Hornsby in *The Three Sisters*. Marius Goring
shared the burden of Hamlet by playing occasionally for Maurice Evans
when the play was given in its entirety.

During this season David Ffolkes was chiefly responsible for costumes
and scenery with the exception of *Othello*, when much of the McKnight
Kauffer production was used.

One of the most important items of the 1935-6 season was a revival
of *Peer Gynt* with William Devlin as Peer. There was a new translation
by R. Ellis Roberts, and Ase was played by Florence Kahn, the wife
of Max Beerbohm. Eric Newton did the settings. I have already spoken
of Ion Swinley's Button Moulder. At the Wells the play was given in
its entirety which must have been extremely interesting, and all who saw
it agreed that, as with *Hamlet*, the full version was infinitely superior
to a shortened one.

'St Helena', 1935-6

Keneth Kent as Napoleon, with, on his right, Ion Swinley and William Devlin ;
on his left, Vivienne Bennett. Unusually for the Old Vic, this was a new play, by
R. C. Sherriff and Jeanne de Casalis.

Another very interesting event was the production of a new play
by R. C. Sherriff and Jeanne de Casalis on the subject of Napoleon in
the last phase. The authors contrived to put a man of substance on the
stage, and not a pasteboard figure. Frequently famous men, given
dramatic life, do all their great deeds off-stage, and we find them just
dull fellows like ourselves. This Emperor did not depend on his well-
known cocked hat, his straddled legs, and hand thrust into white waist-
coat. It is said that Napoleon took lessons in deportment from the great
actor Talma, and that that is where he learned his characteristic tricks !

Keneth Kent created a real person and was particularly successful
when Napoleon was driving his staff crazy with his gardening schemes.
Leo Genn and Cecil Trouncer exhibited qualities which were dead right
for the Old Vic. The play was successful enough to be transferred to
Daly's Theatre (since demolished) and Michael MacOwan took over the
next production.

XIII

Guthrie Returns

' Tyrone Guthrie has come back to us.'   Such a *cri-de-coeur* in the sober
Annual Report is not without significance.   The prodigal returns, the
fatted calf is slain.   In other words the Green Leaflet is put into the
stewpot and the rigidity of its bones comes out considerably softened.
No longer was the producer tied down to dates ; his unsuccessful
efforts could now be curtailed, and his winners allowed to run their course.
From henceforth only the next production is announced, with one or
two future ones vaguely promised, and the public referred to the daily
Press for further information.   Another innovation was the reduction
in the size of the permanent repertory company with the result that
special engagements could be made for certain parts.   This had the
obvious advantage of a more balanced and perfect casting, but on the
other hand it struck at the root of the repertory company as such.   One
cannot pretend that when Lilian Baylis drifted into Shakespeare in 1914
she had any high-flown principle in mind of founding a permanent
repertory company.   That expediency grew out of her general plan for
entertaining the masses.   When she was only able to offer very meagre
salaries the prospect of eight or nine months' certain work lured many who
would otherwise have considered the engagement uneconomical.   By
this time the salary list had risen considerably and the long-term offer was
not so necessary from that point of view, but the ideal of a company
working together for most of a year and often longer was an ideal not
to be abandoned lightly.   However, time was to show that Guthrie's
innovation was of a temporary nature, and the work he did under Lilian
Baylis, and when he himself became Administrator after her death was
remarkable for its vitality and fine achievement.

The opening play, *Love's Labour's Lost*, does not seem to have attracted.
I did not see it, but judging by a production of Guthrie's that I saw at
the Westminster in 1932 it must have been delightful.

RUTH GORDON

This brilliant American player appeared in Guthrie's production
of *The Country Wife* which broke all attendance records at the
Old Vic in the 1936-7 season.

That Rabelaisian Restoration comedy *The Country Wife* followed and
broke all records, and had it not been previously booked for production
in America it might have run the whole season. Ernest Thesiger who
was Sparkish tells me that an unprecedented advertisement appeared
in the ' Agony ' column of *The Times* offering two guineas for a stall at
the Old Vic on any night !

Ben Greet once said that Lilian Baylis had a way with her ; well, I
fancy Guthrie must have had a way with him ! How else did the
Wycherley wench push past the Governors and arrive on the stage of
The Royal Victoria Coffee Music Hall ? The play was brilliantly cast
—up to the hilt as far as drawing power and ability went : Edith Evans,

'THE COUNTRY WIFE', 1936-7
'The play was brilliantly cast' : seated, Ruth Gordon, Kate Cutler, Ursula Jeans,
Edith Evans, Iris Hoey, Eileen Peel ; middle, standing, Freda Jackson, Patrick Barr,
Richard Goolden, Alec Clunes, Ernest Thesiger ; top, James Dale, Michael Redgrave.
Oliver Messel designed the costumes.

Michael Redgrave, Ursula Jeans and, of course, Ruth Gordon. None
of us who saw her do the 'Letter' scene will ever forget it.

How shocked a student of the archaeologically correct school must
have been at the idea of dressing *As You Like It* à la Watteau. How
scandalized I should have been in my Benson days ! And yet how
successful it was when done by Esmé Church for the spring production
of 1937. The eighteenth-century coat and breeches made Rosalind's
disguise quite reasonable, and the placing of Celia from time to time
on such a swing as one can see on the fans in the Wallace Collection
was particularly happy. What young actress in the part of Celia has
not suffered from the long lapses that dear William has permitted her
to have on her hands with naught to do, while Rosalind and Orlando
indulge in scintillating backchat ? At an Open Air performance in

Regent's Park she can explore the blue distances while plucking wild flowers, but in a theatre in a forest of paint and canvas what can she do better than gently swing and dream of Oliver, and hope that one day he will become a reformed character ?

What an enchanting creature Edith Evans made of Rosalind ! Witty, charming and boyish. Rosalind's high jinks can so easily become a cross between coyness and a heavy gambol. It goes without saying that Edith Evans avoided this easily enough. She made one think of something that once was said of Ellen Terry . . . ' she speaks the words as if they have just come into her mind '.

Orlando (well played by Michael Redgrave) is not a role that has much sparkle for the audience and there is only one way to play him : that is, to give oneself utterly to the part of Rosalind. He is her foil, and if he fulfils that function well he will at least win the hearts of the audience. Milton Rosmer was Touchstone and James Dale Jaques.

Hamlet again—this time with Laurence Olivier as the Prince. What is the magic in this play that makes the devotee willing to see it over and over again, and, although knowing every turn and twist of the story and most of the words, to be thrilled every time ? Olivier's performance was provocative. As an actor that is part of his excellence always. I found him intensely interesting, a shade too acrobatic, and belonging to that class of Hamlet that makes it not so easy to accept ' How all occasions do inform against me.' It takes a Forbes-Robertson and a Gielgud to explain that side of Hamlet's character.

Guthrie has in two productions made his players the kind that I have seen in Bruges, and years ago in the Midlands, playing in booths of wood and canvas. This time their entrance with their gaily coloured cart and tawdry dresses was fun, but I don't believe such a troupe would have been invited to perform in the castle of Elsinore any more than the ones I saw would be found giving a performance at Sandringham. The advice that Hamlet gives to the actors is needed by most of us but I doubt whether he would have attempted the task of correcting the faults of such indifferent performers. And excellent as Marius Goring was on Guthrie's lines, would the Prince have welcomed him as an old friend ?

One small point in the stage management which I criticized was the Queen's plunge to death off the top of a high rostrum. It was a stunt fall which took the mind off the action of the drama which at that moment should be swift and consecutive.

The afternoon I saw the play, an actor of no little renown was sitting beside me in the dark of Miss Baylis's box. Leaning towards me he whispered, ' You know what is wrong with this ? ' and answering himself

LAURENCE OLIVIER AND JESSICA TANDY
As Henry and the French Princess in *Henry V*, 1936-7.

as he lightly touched his breast, ' There's no heart in it ! '   At the time
I was amused inwardly, for I thought it rather a tinsel phrase—the
kind of thing that Fred Terry might have said if Harlequin had
appeared as the Scarlet Pimpernel ; but now I am not certain that
there was not a germ of truth in it.   It was a brilliant but not a moving
performance.

Twelfth Night I did not see, but I heard on all sides of Olivier's *tour
de force* as Sir Toby Belch.

The play that followed was *Henry V* and I was swept back into the
Vic as the French King Charles VI, with which I doubled the Archbishop of Canterbury.   Guthrie set himself to debunk this character
and the well-known ' honey-bee ' speech which, oddly enough, con-

EMLYN WILLIAMS AND ANGELA BADDELEY
As Richard and Lady Anne in *Richard III*, 1937-8.

sidering Shakespeare's knowledge of natural history, is not good bee-lore. If any citizens of Canterbury who held in their hearts the revered memory of the original Archbishop, Henry Chichele, saw the performance, they must have been scandalized. It was all very good fun, but I am not confident that I really satisfied the producer. Olivier directed the scene to the same tune in a different key when he made his famous film of *Henry V*. Of his own performance it is not necessary to speak as all the world has seen it on the ' pictures '. His success in the play was no less striking.

Guthrie's colourful production was achieved simply enough by great banners suspended at an angle from the sides of the stage. Henry's figure, rising suddenly from the midst of a great crowd of soldiers to

K

'MEASURE FOR MEASURE', 1937-8
Stephen Murray as the Duke, and Marie Ney as Isabella in the closing scene. In this play Emlyn Williams, as Angelo, made his Old Vic debut.

speak the 'Once more unto the breach' speech, was most effective. Another moment that thrilled me was when on the parting of traverse curtains the Princess Katharine and her companion Alice (irresistibly played by Jessica Tandy and Ivy St Helier) were borne forward on a kind of palanquin on the shoulders of half a dozen stalwart men. And one does not forget the restoration of the Burgundy speech, faultlessly spoken by Leo Genn.

When I played the French King in my own production, I introduced a game of chess with a little hunchback. Guthrie suggested that this time it should be cards. I have been told that playing-cards were invented to beguile this mad old monarch, but have no proof of it. One day while I was copying some cards of the period in the Victoria and Albert Museum, a girl at the same table upset a bottle of Indian ink (forbidden in the museum !) across an illustration in a book of Persian art. I shall never forget her cry of horror—or the unexpected gentleness of the curator.

It was at the first night of this play (*Henry V*) that Guthrie says he had his only real row with Lilian Baylis. It took place in the famous box. The dress rehearsal had finished at 4 a.m. Without consulting

'TWELFTH NIGHT', 1936-7
Left to right : Jessica Tandy (Viola), Laurence Olivier (Sir Toby Belch), Alec Guinness (Sir Andrew Aguecheek).

her Guthrie had arranged that the whole company (on this occasion nearly a hundred strong) should be sent home in cabs at the expense of the management. Cabs were an old bone of contention. Generous in big things, Lilian Baylis could be almost incredibly close over small expenses, and saw no good reason why, if the last trains and trams had gone, the company should not be prepared to walk home. 'Though technically in the wrong,' says Guthrie, 'I thought I was morally right. So did she, but very properly she was not going to let me get away with it and kept me standing behind her in the shadows of the crimson curtain while she administered a sibilant dressing down in devastating asides while she greeted members of the audience over the edge of the box.'

Before the opening of the next season the successful experiment of a drama festival at Buxton was made. The plays given were *Measure for Measure*, Ibsen's *Ghosts*, and Shaw's *Pygmalion* in which Diana Wynyard was the Eliza Doolittle. This was the opening play at the Old Vic that autumn. I was present at the first night of the play at His Majesty's Theatre when Mrs Patrick Campbell spoke the notorious exit line for the first time. But it 'goes' with the audience just as well now, which

MARIUS GORING AND BEATRIX LEHMANN
In *The Witch of Edmonton*, 1936-7 ; the first play produced at the Old Vic by the
French producer, Michel Saint-Denis.

proves that the effect is made by Eliza's unexpected reversion to type
rather than by an expletive to which we are all now thoroughly inured
in this world of progress ! The cast at the Vic included Robert Morley,
Mark Dignam, Jean Cadell, Stephen Murray, and Jay Laurier.

In Esmé Church's production of *Ghosts*, which did not go to the Vic
but to the Vaudeville, Marie Ney is reported to have scored as Mrs
Alving. She returned to the company to play Isabella in *Measure for
Measure* to the Angelo of Emlyn Williams. That, I think, was this
actor's first appearance at the Old Vic, and he only stayed for the
following production, *Richard III*. It is a pity for the Vic's sake that
fate did not send him earlier in his career when he could have afforded
the time for a whole season. His fine flair for the theatre and his
unusual personality, rather like one of his native Welsh mines with little
on the surface to indicate the flaming passion in its heart, might have
achieved greatly.

I wish I had seen his Richard. I asked Angela Baddeley, who was
the Lady Anne in that production, what she remembered about his
performance. I think she used the word 'thrilling', which after all
might be said of many things, but it was the expression in her eyes that
told me that he was more than that. I thought that this was Miss

Baddeley's only appearance at the Old Vic, but she played the Duke of Gloucester in a Ben Greet production of the same play when she was nine years old. How did the management evade the child licence regulations? Well, Lilian Baylis was an adept in keeping the L.C.C. at bay and yet remaining on the friendliest terms with them!

In the reception given to *Measure for Measure* on this occasion one sees an example of the fickleness of the theatregoing public. Guthrie's 1934 production had drawn all London. This one did not do well. Now why? It was very well cast and must have been well played and well produced.

The Annual Report in speaking of the next production says that Olivier gave a remarkable performance as Macbeth to which he had given months of careful study. I can well believe that. He does not trifle with his job. The Australian-born actress Judith Anderson was the Lady Macbeth. The play ran four weeks, and was then transferred to the New Theatre. But before that happened, a real tragedy had overtaken the Old Vic.

I have spoken already of the superstition that hag-rides the play of *Macbeth* with disaster. It is a mistake to dwell on these things whether one accepts them or rejects them, but this particular revival in 1937 brought in its wake catastrophes which cannot be ignored. First of all Michel Saint-Denis, who was producing on this occasion, encountered unexpected difficulties in working on the Old Vic stage; then Olivier developed a bad chill which made it imperative to postpone the opening date from the Tuesday to the Friday. Postponement had never happened at the Old Vic before. If anyone was ill Lilian Baylis promptly got some old member of the company to rush into the breach. On this occasion she made an exception and philosophically accepted the postponement. She was far from well at the time and had been battling against ill health for three or four years—a combat that she knew she was losing. But for her anxiety about the future of the theatres she would have been quite content to die. She said so more than once to her friends. On the Tuesday evening she intended to return to the theatre to do some more work. While at home she suffered a shock— no matter what, except that it had nothing to do with her work; but its effect made it impossible for her to go back to the Old Vic that night. The Lilian Baylis that we all knew was never to go there again. That night she telephoned Father Andrew to put off an appointment for the next day. He offered to come to her instead, but she would not hear of it. 'I should hate you to come and see me. I'm not fit to be seen.' In answer to his 'God bless you', came the words, 'I was just waiting for you to say that.'

XIV

Lilian Baylis

WHAT sort of a woman was Lilian Baylis ? It is misleading to say that she was stout. She was thickset, but not fat. She was about five foot four inches high, and moved lightly. She had been trained as a dancer at one time, and was not a little proud of her lightness of movement. She had pretty, soft brown hair and gentle, rather weak, eyes. She always wore spectacles, and all who met her were conscious of her slightly crooked mouth, a feature that has been imitated many times in the telling of those stories which, though characteristic and even funny, tend to obscure the real woman and are often quite untrue. Beatrice Wilson once told me of an incident that occurred during a holiday in South Wales. She and Lilian Baylis were bathing in a very rough sea. Miss Wilson was swimming out some distance when her friend called to her to come back. On reaching the shore she said, ' Why did you call me back, Lilian ? I was all right.' ' Look at my mouth,' said Lilian. ' It's crooked.   Once when I was a young girl in South Africa I swam out in a much worse sea than this and got into difficulties. Wave after wave was battering one side of my face. I lost my nerve and then passed out. After I was rescued I found that my face was quite crooked—as if I'd had a stroke. Gradually it recovered. All except my mouth.' Miss Wilson said that she always felt embarrassed and ashamed when people mimicked Lilian Baylis. ' I can hear her saying, " Look at my mouth. It's crooked." '

Many who knew her speak of her cockney accent. It was not cockney but South African and she took some pains to correct it. In the early days she was notoriously careless about her appearance, but latterly she allowed herself to be dressed by a friend who was skilled in such matters.

Tyrone Guthrie thus describes her :

' Hundreds of theatregoers must be familiar with the dumpy

LILIAN BAYLIS IN HER BOX
A familiar sight to Old Vic first-night audiences.

motherly spectacled figure that sat in her Box on every first-night for
so many years—in a sable cape lined with bright mauve over a black
taffeta coat with beautiful painted enamel buttons. These had
belonged to Mrs Stirling, an old actress who had played the Nurse
to Ellen Terry's Juliet.'

Lord Lytton who nine years before had become chairman of the
Governing Body called her 'a masterful woman of genius'. Certainly
there were times when differences of opinion occurred at the meetings
and she would become engaged in heated argument with one or other of
the Governors. She would get very excited and explosive, giving
expression to vehement opinions at the top of her voice. But there was
never any malice in her outbursts. They were always in defence of some
principle which she held sacred, and the storms would subside as quickly

TWELFTH NIGHT CEREMONY
Lilian Baylis cuts the cake in the presence of the company.

as they arose. Yes, she could be unruly and stubborn, impatient of the considerations of finance, but her faith and optimism triumphed over all practical difficulties.

'It was at such times', says Guthrie, 'that one perceived the lightning behind those motherly spectacles, the tigress encased in Mrs Stirling's buttons. Then it was easy to picture the Lilian of an earlier day swarming up the ladder to the flies (a perpendicular ladder flush with the wall) during the Garden scene in *Faust* to eject a drunken fireman. "He was blaspheming against God, my dear, in the middle of that lovely quiet bit." She fought him in the flies and forced him down the ladder in front of her, praying to God to give her strength to hold him if he lost his footing on the rungs.'

Guthrie says he saw her go up to the gallery when some misguided philanthropist had brought a party of prostitutes from a Home. They were laughing in the wrong places and creating a disturbance by calling out. 'You shut up, you poor stupid rough women!' exclaimed Lilian. 'Behave yourselves properly or I'll bang your heads together.' Silence!

and down she came. ' Poor dear fallen women,' she said with tears in her eyes. ' It seems a shame they can't enjoy themselves.'

Lilian Baylis was born in London in 1874. Her father was Edward Newton Baylis and he married a younger sister of Emma Cons, known as ' Liebe ' Cons. They brought a large family into the world. Neither she nor her musical husband was very practical and in 1891 they decided to try their luck in South Africa. The whole family was musical so they formed a concert party and toured the country in ox-wagons, playing in the raw new towns, in farms and settlements, and wherever an audience could be collected. Lilian Baylis had been a pupil of the violinist Carrodus and had appeared as a child prodigy at the old St James's Hall. Her musical ability was greater than that of the rest of the family, and so was her efficiency. Her mother seems to have found plenty of time for enjoying herself, but little for looking after her family. Lilian seems to have taken on that responsibility together with many others, including the planning of the family itinerary. She also seems to have spared moments from her busy life to help friends in the delivery of their illegitimate babies. In a new country where the conventions had scarcely established themselves and where so much was exciting and adventurous, to one who enjoyed life so wholeheartedly there must have been pitfalls, but Lilian took them all in her stride and learned from constant experience how to manage the advances of amorous pioneers. ' Indeed,' affirms Evelyn Williams to whom I am indebted for this sketch of the South African days, 'many of Lilian Baylis's reminiscences of those days had a Rabelaisian flavour ! '

In spite of the touring activities and all else, she found time to found the first school of dancing on the Rand and many a South African distinguished in later life had learned his first position under Lilian's watchful eye.   There can be no doubt that this hard-working, responsible apprenticeship in her young days shaped her character and strengthened it for the strenuous battle that was before her.

In 1895 she was seriously ill and Aunt Emma cabled an invitation for her to return to England to recuperate.   The girl found her aunt was doing too much—Emma Cons had many activities besides the Old Vic—and she offered to help her with work at the theatre.   Evelyn Williams suspects that Lilian Baylis was somewhat bored by the change of surroundings.   Emma Cons consented to the arrangement, little realizing that she had installed a permanent tornado in her theatre. No more was heard of Lilian Baylis's return to South Africa !   Let it be remembered that when she came back to England in 1895 she was only twenty-one years old, and when later she was officially appointed manager of the Old Vic in 1898, she was twenty-four.   Her salary was one pound a week, to be raised to thirty bob if she proved her worth. However, ' her gay, earthy, vivid life in South Africa had broadened her sympathies.   She assessed men and women as individuals judging them skilfully for their fitness to do a particular job '.   I have but recently learned of this strange kaleidoscope of her early life from Evelyn Williams and I deeply regret that I was unaware of it when I was working at the Old Vic.   I am convinced that it would have been a great help to me in my relations with my manager, revealing much that I did not understand or appreciate at the time.

That she was conscious of her lack of intellectual background is another point that Miss Williams makes, and that was why she was always willing to give her lieutenants their head, and to ask experts for advice.   The legends of stinginess and narrow religious outlook are not important.   She paid poorly because with a limited income it was the only thing to do.   By the charters of the theatres she was a paid servant like anyone else.   Any surplus—and how rarely there was one—went into better productions, or into the bank to be lost in an ocean of debt.   Perhaps those debts should never have been

incurred. Had they not, there would have been no Old Vic, no Sadler's Wells.

Shortly after her death a pen portrait of her appeared in the *Observer* under the signature of St John Ervine. This much upset an old friend of hers in the person of Sir Hugh Walpole. But he found to his surprise that many agreed with St John Ervine and thought that she was too careful about money, a prude in morals, ill-educated, conceited, a fanatical egoist. On the other hand there were some who had seen her only as an affectionate, humorous, faithful friend. Some saw her as a saint, some thought her unique, and one or two hated her with that vehemence that only really remarkable people can arouse. Two things were clear and incontestable—one, that she had done against all odds a most remarkable piece of work, and the other that she was a unique person. The interesting thing in studying her is to reconcile the differences. They are so opposite and yet in all probability they are true. She was a brute, a devil, a tyrant, ignorant, selfish, what you will ; but she was also a great, courageous, inspired figure, and she was an untidy, ugly, affectionate, divinely inspired *gamine* as well, who had the power to arouse tenderness and affection.

'Once,' wrote Walpole, 'she took me into her office for ten minutes. "I am so tired, dear. As soon as you are gone I am going to pray for a bit more physique. I have got a rotten body and that's the truth of it." "Do you think you will get it if you pray for it?" I asked her. "Oh, of course," she said, "if it is right for me to have it, and it is right for me just now, I have such a terrible lot to do." "That's rather like dictating to God," I said. "Oh, well He understands me dear," she answered. "Perhaps He may even see through you," I suggested. "So long as He helps the Old Vic, dear," she answered, "He can see through me as much as He likes."'

One other thing Walpole said about her work at the two theatres and it was this: 'Whenever I come away after a performance I feel a kind of creative happiness that has been shared by all.'

I have always appreciated Father Andrew's comparison of Lilian Baylis to St Teresa of Spain. 'Her hatred of humbug and her direct approach to God were very reminiscent of the Spanish saint, though in all probability she had never read her Life.'

St Teresa of Avila, it will be remembered, travelled about the country founding religious houses of her Order. The journeys were arduous and often entailed great hardship, and no less fraught with difficulties was the undertaking at the journey's end. Once in despair she cried aloud to God, 'No wonder you have so many enemies when you treat your friends so badly!' 'In the same kind of way,' says Father Andrew, 'Lilian Baylis would exclaim: "You have got me into this difficulty; you must get me out of it."'

And had she been conscious on that Thursday morning in November, she might have said with St Teresa, 'My Lord, these houses are not mine, they are yours: all that I could do is done. You must see to them now.'

XV

The Storm Threatens

LET me confess at once that I do not like Mendelssohn's incidental music to *A Midsummer Night's Dream*—that is, when it is played as such. I think I may have had too much of it in the Benson company, especially as in those days the 'Spring Song' and 'The Bees' Wedding' were added to the score, not to mention T. S. Cooke's 'Over Hill, Over Dale,' sung by the first fairy. Worst of all Oberon's exquisite speech, 'I know a bank where the wild thyme blows', was sung to C. E. Horn's music by two well-developed fairies obviously of the female sex. Oh, those muslin-clad fairies from the bottom of the garden and the suburban dancing school! One has to sacrifice, I am willing to admit, the entrance music of the Clowns with its ass's bray, but the Wedding March is too redolent of confetti and old satin slippers to adorn a sixteenth-century masque.

However, when Guthrie revived the play in 1937 at Christmas time, with décor by Oliver Messel, and the fairies were straight out of an early Victorian ballet and of the Mendelssohn period, then the music was delightful, as indeed was the whole production. Helpmann as Oberon, looking like some strange, sinister stag-beetle, was indeed a spirit of another sort. His speech and his movement, as one would expect, were beautiful. Vivien Leigh as his consort looked like one of those delicious coloured prints of the period. Ralph Richardson as Bottom was, if anything, better than before, and the lovers were in the safe hands of Agnes Lauchlan, Alexis Franoe, Stephen Murray and Anthony Quayle. The fairies were undertaken by the Vic-Wells Ballet under the direction of Ninette de Valois and were perfectly attuned to the spirit of Guthrie's production.

I saw Richardson play a darkie in an oleographic play called *Oroonoko* at the Malvern Festival. I thought then that he would one day make a good Othello. But when I saw him play it in the next production, with

RALPH RICHARDSON AS BOTTOM
In Guthrie's enchanting and memorable production of *A Midsummer Night's Dream*, 1937-8.

Laurence Olivier as Iago, I was disappointed. The performance had
many good qualities but it never caught fire. I was reminded of
Forbes-Robertson in the part. His performance was one of great
dignity and restrained power. He did not tear a passion to tatters, but
one was never in doubt that a reserve of great power was held in leash.
I found his Othello more moving than any I have seen. No one can show
restraint in film work better than Ralph Richardson, but that particular
virtue should be used with discretion in the theatre.

James Bridie made his bow as an author at the Old Vic with a new
play *The King of Nowhere*. Unfortunately it coincided with the Munich
crisis. It was followed by *Coriolanus* with Lewis Casson as producer and
Sybil Thorndike as Volumnia. Bruce Winston did the décor. I
deeply regret that I was unable to see the revival. Olivier must have

158

ROBERT HELPMANN AS OBERON
In *A Midsummer Night's Dream*, 1937-8. Décor and costume by
Oliver Messel.

been extremely interesting as Coriolanus. Terence O'Brien returned
after several years' absence to play Cominius, and Cecil Trouncer
Menenius.

So came to an end a season that will be remembered by all who hold
the Old Vic and Sadler's Wells theatres in their hearts. I believe Emma
Cons on her deathbed said to her niece, 'Look after the children'.
Lilian Baylis, in the performances she arranged under the L.C.C. scheme,
did not neglect that wish, but she nourished two emblematic children as
well in the two theatres of her creation, and she gave the whole of her life
to tending their growth.

Before she died she had largely departmentalized the work of the two
theatres. Tyrone Guthrie had been appointed Director of Drama,
Ninette de Valois Director of Ballet, and a committee of the producers

'SHE STOOPS TO CONQUER', 1938-9

Left to right : George Benson (Tony Lumpkin), Margaret Yarde (Mrs Hardcastle),
Frank Napier (Sir Charles Marlow), Edward Chapman (Mr Hardcastle),
Ursula Jeans (Miss Hardcastle), John Mills (Young Marlow), Pamela Brown
(Miss Neville), Anthony Nicholls (Hastings).

and conductors of opera under the chairmanship of Sumner Austin was
largely in control of operatic affairs ; general administration had for
some years been entrusted increasingly to Bruce Worsley and Evelyn
Williams. It was now decided to interfere with this system as little as
possible, and the work was carried on without serious difficulty.

The plays chosen for the second Buxton season in the summer of 1938
were *Hamlet* in modern dress with Alec Guinness as the Prince, *The
Rivals*, *Trelawny of the Wells*, and *Henry V*.

That was the autumn of the Munich crisis and things began to be
difficult for the theatres. The Old Vic opened in late September with
Trelawny of the Wells, and in October *Hamlet* was given.

Hamlet at the beginning of the season instead of the end ! *Hamlet*
in modern dress ! Surely the trumpets of Joshua were not more
shattering ? And yet the walls of the Old Vic still stood up.

'THE TAMING OF THE SHREW', 1938-9

Roger Livesey (Petruchio) and Frederick Bennett (Grumio), with their 'horse' in
Tyrone Guthrie's gay production of the play. Ursula Jeans played opposite Roger
Livesey as Katharina, and Robert Helpmann appeared as the Tailor. Décor and
costumes were by Roger Furse.

Since Sir Barry Jackson's bold experiment with *Hamlet* at the Kingsway
Theatre we have grown accustomed to modern-dress representations
of the classics. I have always found such innovations invigorating
and helpful. They shed new light on the words that have become too
familiar and reduce the more purple patches to their proper tints.
There is little doubt that the fellowship of players at the Globe theatre
thought of Hamlet's mother as a person looking much like Queen
Elizabeth and Polonius as a caricature of such a statesman as the great
Lord Burghley. Certainly the boy who played Hamlet at the Kingsway
—Colin Keith-Johnston—made one think of the then Prince of Wales,
and the Polonius might have been Lord Balfour. Yes, it was an exciting,
splendid thing to do at the Old Vic. It gave the dear old haunted place
a good shaking up !

He whom one might call the Bard's devil's advocate, in the person

SYBIL THORNDIKE AND LAURENCE OLIVIER
In *Coriolanus*, 1937-8.

of Bernard Shaw, followed with his *Man and Superman*, though the scene in Hell itself was omitted.

This company stayed at the Old Vic until Christmas and in January set off on a Mediterranean tour under the auspices of the British Council. They took a wide range of plays : *Hamlet, Henry V, Viceroy Sarah, Trelawny of the Wells, Man and Superman, The Rivals, I Have Been Here Before*, and a play called *Libel*—not, as one might imagine, to satisfy the fleshpots of Shepheard's Hotel, but at the request of the Egyptian authorities, as it was a work set for an important examination !

That Christmas Guthrie revived his very happy production of *A*

Midsummer Night's Dream with Helpmann again as Oberon, Edward Chapman in place of Richardson as Bottom, and John Mills as Puck. Mills stayed on to play Young Marlow in *She Stoops to Conquer*. Roger Livesey and Ursula Jeans rejoined. They appeared as Petruchio and Katharina in *The Taming of the Shrew*, and other parts. Helpmann played the Tailor. *An Enemy of the People* was the other play.

The third Buxton season opened hopefully in 1939 but the war-cloud was gathering. Robert Donat played Dick Dudgeon in *The Devil's Disciple* and Romeo in *Romeo and Juliet*, and Constance Cummings played the leading role in *St Joan*. I am told that Donat did some of his finest work in Goldsmith's *The Good-Natured Man*. Unfortunately these productions never reached the Old Vic because, as we all know, the cloud burst in September and the second World War was upon us. From now until the starting of the new Old Vic in 1944 the history of the theatre becomes involved to a degree.

During that first strange year when the world seemed to be holding its breath—when we expected the cataclysm which persistently hung fire until it took on the unreality of a mirage—both theatres were closed and the companies went on tour. Then in the spring of 1940 Tyrone Guthrie boldly reopened the Old Vic with a revival of *King Lear*. It was to have what is called an all-star cast, but, if I may say so, it was a good deal better than that. Lewis Casson produced the play in association with Harley Granville-Barker, but Barker was unable to take command until the last ten days or so. Into that all too short period he crushed a month's work. Fortunately Casson's schooling had put us all on the right road and Barker lost no time in whipping us from a jogtrot into a canter.

Youngsters often ask me in what way Granville-Barker was a great producer. It is not an easy matter to answer that question, any more than one can convey the thrill of Irving's acting, or the miracle that was Ellen Terry. Roughly, one might say that Barker worked from the inside to the outside. He had an exceptional instinct for what was theatrically effective but never got it by theatrical means. It had to be won by mental clarity and emotional truth—in fact the very opposite to the method of most producers. Besides his intellectual attainments he had gone through the rough and tumble of an actor's training and knew to a hair's breadth what an actor could put up with and how he could best be handled. I have known him change readings and positions from day to day, without explaining why he did it, on purpose to break down the inhibitions of some actor, and at last, out of the subconscious if you will, would emerge the right way of doing it. It could be an agony to a sensitive actor, but hard training never hurt anyone. Before my wife left the stage proper to become a diseuse, she played Alice in Granville-Barker's play *The Voysey Inheritance*. She found the part very difficult, as indeed it is, and Barker dragooned her not a little, but finally got the result that he wanted ; at the end of the last dress rehearsal he kissed her hand with a courteous gesture that seemed to beg forgiveness for the pain and anguish of creation.

When producing a play he always had the whole thing at his fingers' ends at the first rehearsal. That the stage management was always fixed to the last movement goes without saying, but he also knew the whole background of the play, and what each character should have in his or her mind. I did experience one exception. That was in the last ten minutes of *Lear*. Many of Shakespeare's final acts present difficulties from a stage management point of view. There are usually a number of characters to be dealt with and, in this play, not a few corpses. For some reason Barker had not been able to visualize those ultimate positions. Late one night, or rather early one morning, he came up on the stage, took off his coat and moved us hither and thither like pawns on a chess-board. The perspiration stood on his forehead before he got our complicated movements into the pattern that satisfied him.

Latterly I think he was inclined to work his cast too hard up to the last moment. The result was that we still had the scaffolding up at the first performance. I noticed this particularly in the production of his own plays, *The Voysey Inheritance* at Sadler's Wells and *Waste* at the Westminster. No doubt it was caused by the time factor (how seldom is there enough time in preparing a production), and by a final effort to drag us up to a standard of perfection which our shortcomings denied him.

John Gielgud was the Lear and I have already spoken of his performance in that part in my own production. How it came out on this occasion I am unable to judge. It had undoubtedly gained in stature in many ways, though perhaps losing a little in others. I am not sure that the Tudor costumes and setting helped him. One of the most arresting and brilliant performances was the Edmund of Jack Hawkins—a fine foil to Robert Harris's romantic Edgar. Fay Compton, Jessica Tandy, Cathleen Nesbitt, Stephen Haggard, Nicholas Hannen, and Andrew Cruickshank made up a splendid team which worked well together. The Old Vic casts a magic spell of co-operation over its inmates. That luxurious weed called snobbery which sometimes creeps into the West End theatre cannot survive in the Waterloo Road.

In confirmation of Lear's cry ' I kill'd the slave that was a-hanging thee,' an officer says,' 'Tis true, my lords, he did.' Young James Donald was the officer, and since then he has established himself in plays by

'A MIDSUMMER NIGHT'S DREAM', 1937-8

The lovers quarrel : a scene from Guthrie's exquisite ' tuppence coloured ' production,
accompanied, appropriately, by Mendelssohn's incidental music.

Noel Coward, Cocteau, and George Bernard Shaw. For myself, I
stumbled about in the part of Albany not too happily. I hug the belief
that it is not a very satisfactorily drawn character. James Agate
wrote of my performance that Albany was asking to be cuckolded !

King Lear was followed by *The Tempest* which was produced by George
Devine and Marius Goring with décor by Oliver Messel. The scenery
had a peculiar loveliness—misty and mysterious, like the bottom of the
sea. The ship was based on a medieval picture : the figures larger than
the ship. The effect was delightful to look at and in some ways good fun.
The ship pitched enough to make the characters all seasick but it did
not actually assist the dramatic effect aimed at by the author, who has
sketched that little scene with an economy of masterly strokes.

Gielgud was the Prospero, Jack Hawkins Caliban, and Jessica Tandy
Miranda. Marius Goring was the Ariel. He is too skilled an actor not
to give an interesting performance of any part, but I found him a thought
heavy. I suppose the ideal Ariel was the boy of Shakespeare's day
trained specially for that kind of part. Leslie French, when he played
it, though not a boy, had the great advantage of expert singing
knowledge and ballet training.

'KING LEAR', SPRING 1940

Left to right : Robert Harris (Edgar), Cathleen Nesbitt (Goneril), Harcourt Williams (Albany). In the foreground, Jack Hawkins as Edmund. The play was produced at the Old Vic by Lewis Casson in association with Harley Granville-Barker.

XVI

The Storm Breaks

IN the autumn of 1940 the mirage faded and the cataclysm was upon us in the shape of the September raids.   It soon became evident that it was impossible to manage the complicated affairs of the Old Vic and Sadler's Wells from London.   Sadler's Wells had been commandeered as a clearing house for homeless refugees from bombed areas, which involved the staff in twenty-four hour duties and responsibilities.   They were never free to attend to their own jobs, and got very little sleep. Communication with the companies in various parts of the country became virtually impossible.   Posts were disorganized and the delays on the telephone made it almost useless.   The only solution was to move the headquarters to somewhere in the north.   Burnley was chosen as a convenient centre for this purpose and the move was executed in a few crowded days.   The experiment not only saved the situation but proved eminently successful, largely due to the sympathy with the project shown by the proprietors of the Victoria Theatre, Burnley.   What a comforting coincidence that that temporary refuge should bear the same name, so redolent of peaceful, solid, unalarming days !

'In the theatre, as elsewhere,' writes Tyrone Guthrie of those times, ' this has been a period when values have had to be revised, old methods scrapped, new ones improvised.   Tours to places, which in twenty-five years have had no professional entertainment other than " the pictures " and exceedingly cheap vaudeville, have been made financially possible by C.E.M.A., the medium through which the British Treasury, for the first time since the Tudors, had made manifest a belief that the theatre in particular is a necessity to a nation which wishes to consider itself civilized.'

Professor Dent says that the Old Vic company was the first to co-operate with C.E.M.A., which, under its present title of the Arts Council

'THE MERCHANT OF VENICE'
Left to right : Felicity Lyster, Jean Forbes-Robertson, Renée Asherson and Pauline Williams—a picture of a wartime touring company production which shows the simple screen sets that were employed.

of Great Britain, has been concerned with the Old Vic and Sadler's Wells organizations ever since.

It was indeed a brave band that kept the flag flying in those troublous times. Joan Cross subordinated her career as a singer to lead the opera. Sumner Austin directed during the first critical months. Lawrance Collingwood and Constant Lambert were conductors of opera and ballet. Ninette de Valois kept the ballet in existence in face of almost insuperable difficulties, with the help of Frederick Ashton.

Sybil Thorndike, Esmé Church, and Lewis Casson led the drama tours, which included the amazing experiment of taking *Macbeth* to small and distant mining centres in Wales. A tour to cover thirty-eight towns in ten weeks was arranged. Frederick Crooke designed a portable setting of two four-fold screens, a proscenium and black surround, and most original costumes of the 1745 period. Casson says it was a compact, hard-working company with much doubling. Sybil Thorndike played the First Witch, as well as Lady Macbeth, and another actress had a busy evening with the Second Witch, Fleance,

ON TOUR IN WARTIME

Sybil Thorndike, Esmé Church and Lewis Casson led the wartime drama tours,
which took great plays, great acting, and the great traditions of the Old Vic into
industrial centres all over Britain.

Lady Macduff and Young Siward ! The company travelled in a bus
and the scenery and staff in a lorry. They played in parish halls,
miners' institutes, sometimes a palatial cinema, once on a stage no
bigger than a ' tablecloth '—but always to full houses and the same
enthusiasm, and, as Casson puts it, ' the same hunger for what we were
bringing '. There is one other name to be added to this roll of honour.
It is that of Bronson Albery who threw open the doors of the New
Theatre to all three companies from time to time.

Lilian Baylis might have preferred to stand a siege in her office on
the Lower Marsh and in doing so she might have been wrong. Who can
tell ? But of this I am certain, she would have been proud of that little
band of Crispian brothers.

The amount of work put out during that Burnley exile is indeed
remarkable. I have counted twenty-four plays sent out on the ' road '
in the most trying circumstances of an unexampled war time. Eight
of these were Shakespearean productions, the rest by Shaw, Chekhov,
Euripides, Goldsmith, Housman, Saroyan, and Robert Ardrey.

'HAMLET', FEBRUARY 1944

Robert Helpmann as Hamlet in the production by Tyrone Guthrie and Michael
Benthall at the New Theatre, London. Left: Frederic Horrey (Rosencrantz),
David Carr (Guildenstern).

For a few months in the autumn of 1940 I was stationed at Manchester
as a member of the B.B.C. Drama Repertory Company and had the
good fortune to see the touring company playing *She Stoops to Conquer*
at Stockport one afternoon. It was a joy to see some decent acting
again. The cast was headed by Esmé Church—who also produced—
Alec Clunes, Sonia Dresdel, and Renée Asherson. Cleverly contrived
screens and draperies supplied the effective scenery. (Oh, Gordon
Craig and William Poel—prophets so absurdly without honour in your
own country—how your works are borrowed even by the simple !) It
was such a jolly, lively performance and it was so refreshing to sit among
a crammed audience so patiently eager for what the theatre alone could
give them. The cinema offers us a good but such a different repast.
And heaven above, what opportunities it has let go by ! Here in that
little theatre at Stockport with the numbing tragedy of war outside it
was glorious to hear such laughter, and the wholehearted, simple
enjoyment took me back to the enthusiasm of the Old Vic audiences.
Later I saw the same company at Altrincham in *Twelfth Night*, with

'OTHELLO', 1942

The Old Vic company at the New Theatre. Left to right : Bernard Miles (Iago), Hermione Hannen (Desdemona), Freda Jackson (Emilia). Frederick Valk appeared in the title role.

one notable addition to the cast in the person of Ernest Milton. He played Sir Andrew Aguecheek. It was an outrageous performance but as clever as be-damned. What the wardrobe master was up to I don't know, for Milton appeared with perfect sang-froid in an Elizabethan doublet and full tights sans trunks. The effect was, of course, like his performance, superbly comic. Such an Aguecheek, however, tipped the balance of the play right over. Malvolio, Toby, and Clown were over-shadowed to a man, and the women fared little better. Perhaps I ought to add that I thoroughly enjoyed the whole evening !

In the following July (1941) I saw Milton play King John at the New Theatre. The company had been reshaped. Sybil Thorndike repeated her moving performance of Constance. Lewis Casson made something extraordinary out of Pandulph. It was the picture of a half-blind, cunning old priest in a body that seemed riddled with disease. It was one of Tyrone Guthrie's wildest productions, and as a wartime effort I thought it a very ingenious one. Lewis Casson seems to have had a hand in it too. It was convenient, no doubt, to cast

Ann Casson as Arthur, but a mistake. As Bernard Shaw wrote of Lena Ashwell in Irving's *Richard III*, ' The Lyceum has by no means emancipated itself from gross superstition. Italian opera itself could go no further in folly than the exhibition of a pretty young actress in tights as Prince Edward.' I made the same mistake myself at the Old Vic. It is not a question of the quality of performance given by either young actress. It is simply that Arthur must be played by a boy. But of course in Ann Casson's case it was a wartime measure and much nicer to have the family touring together in those dark days. I once saw the scene acted by ten-year-old Teddy (son of Gordon) Craig and you will never guess who the gaoler was who heated the irons. ' He ' was Ellen Terry, and she was so good one hardly noticed her !

About a year later, in July 1942, Frederick Valk appeared at the New as Othello. He did not move me ; but at a much later date, after he had left the Old Vic, I saw him as Solness in *The Master Builder* and found it ' frightfully thrilling '. I would like to have seen his Shylock. I was very much struck by Iago as played by Bernard Miles.

In 1942 the Governors of the Old Vic and Sadler's Wells appointed Tyrone Guthrie and Bronson Albery as joint Administrators. Bronson Albery held that position until the May of 1944. He had previously been serving on the Board of Governors for three or four years.

In the Annual Report of 1942 Sir Reginald Rowe speaks of the rising prosperity of the Vic-Wells organization, and speaks with definite assurance of the future financial position. After reading through the Annual Reports covering half a century, that is the first time I have seen a glimmer of such a wildly optimistic statement. What were the causes ? They were the backing and interest given by C.E.M.A. and the Carnegie Trustees, the war conditions, and finally Bronson Albery who, besides placing the New Theatre at the disposal of the three companies on advantageous terms, was responsible for the reopening of the Playhouse Theatre, Liverpool, in November 1942, where the Old Vic was able to organize an interesting list of productions and in a short period to make a great deal of money.

In the summer of 1943 the Playhouse Theatre in London was taken over with the idea, I believe, of making it a temporary home until the Old Vic could be repaired. It opened with a revival of Drinkwater's *Abraham Lincoln*, with Herbert Lomas repeating his fine performance in the title role. That stalwart supporter Russell Thorndike came to play General Grant, and I rushed down from the Garrick where I was acting in *Brighton Rock* to make a brief appearance as General Lee. *The Russians*, a play by Konstantin Simonov, followed in which Freda Jackson scored, and then a new play by Peter Ustinov entitled *Blow*

'KING JOHN', 1941

Abraham Sofaer as the King of France, with the French court. This production by
Tyrone Guthrie and Lewis Casson went on tour after a season at the New Theatre.

MRS CLARK

When the raids began, she accompanied the Old Vic on its wartime tours. She had been selling tickets at the theatre since 1916.

Your Own Trumpet. Neither of these three plays attracted sufficient public and the scheme was abandoned.

The next important event was Guthrie's production of *Hamlet* with Robert Helpmann. This did well in spite of a series of sharp air raids. For such a long part I did not find that Helpmann had enough variety of tone. It is not fair to compare them, but for those of us who had seen his *Hamlet* ballet there had been something so blindingly effective in it—like a flash of forked lightning—that the acted version seemed a shadow of the real thing. Basil Sydney's King was first-rate, so too was the Gravedigger of Gus McNaughton—I doubt if I have seen a better. But I have three bones to pick with Guthrie. Why that transposition of the King and Laertes plot to the graveyard scene, allowing Ophelia but two minutes in which to drown herself and less for the ' wretched Queen ' to discover the fact ? Why, when Hamlet is railing at his own lack of action in comparison with young Fortinbras, have that able-bodied hero standing up above the prince doing nothing ? Why (for the second time on earth !) make the First Player a kind of Crummles whom Hamlet—unless he had a touch of Prince Hal in him—could never have called old friend ? May I say here and now that I have the greatest admiration for Guthrie's work and that I never go to see one of his productions without a feeling of excited expectation, and never take part in one without delight.

In the spring of 1944 there was a tour of Zola's *Thérèse Raquin* renamed *Guilty*, with Flora Robson and Violet Farebrother, which had a season at the Lyric Theatre, Hammersmith.

Guthrie, writing in the Report of 1945, records the death of Sir Reginald Rowe in the January of that year. Sir Reginald, with Lilian Baylis, actually recreated Sadler's Wells. ' Nothing ', writes Guthrie, ' was too large, nothing too small, for him to undertake in the interests of the two theatres. He was completely selfless, and his life was the embodiment of service to the community.' Lord Lytton elsewhere speaks of his robust faith and breezy wit, and the fact that he was as irreplaceable as the woman he had worked with, and by whose side he had stood so stoutly through the calm and storm.

It can have been no easy task gathering up the threads unravelled by the wear and tear of war. Among the helpers and servers must be some perforce who stand less in the limelight. There was Tyrone Guthrie with his inventive Irish genius ; George Chamberlain, now clerk to the Governors and general manager of the Old Vic and Sadler's Wells, whose clear grasp of facts has been of the greatest value, and Annette Prevost, who started as Lilian Baylis's personal secretary and made her home happy during her last years. She is now treasurer of the Old Vic and Sadler's Wells, but says those early days were the happiest. The manager of Sadler's Wells, Bruce Worsley, came to the Old Vic after the first World War which had left him physically shaken. Lilian Baylis with her strong maternal instinct (who was it said she ought to have had a family of children ?) took him under her wing and gave him the work he needed and, what was perhaps more important, her friendship. Finally there was dear Mrs Clark whose beaming face at the box-office window was so familiar to us, and who began selling tickets in the days when the box office was a makeshift affair in one of the boxes. Many years later when the raids began, like the true trouper that she is, she packed her bags, changed her calling, and went off into the wilds shepherding the Old Vic sheep in pastures new.

From this time the three activities, opera, ballet and drama, began to separate into three departments of one organization, which might be compared to a commonwealth of three dominions.

'HENRY IV, PT II', 1945-6
Laurence Olivier as Justice Shallow.

XVII

A New Phoenix

EARLY in 1944, while I was acting in one of Ivor Novello's musical productions, John Burrell called on me in my dressing-room and expounded a scheme that was on foot for carrying on the work of the Old Vic at the New Theatre under the directorship of Tyrone Guthrie, Ralph Richardson, Laurence Olivier and himself. The prospect of joining this new venture fired me with enthusiasm. The financial inducement was not great but good enough. A moderate sum was guaranteed plus a small percentage and for the main body of the company it was to be on an equal basis. Dame Sybil Thorndike, Margaret Leighton, and Joyce Redman were the women ; Nicholas Hannen, George Relph, Michael Warre, and myself were the men. Ralph Richardson and Laurence Olivier shared the leads.

The opening plays were to be *Peer Gynt*, *Richard III*, and *Arms and the Man*, and they were to be given in rotation after the manner of a Continental repertoire. Rehearsals started in the summer and were held in a large empty hall in the National Gallery. It was not a good place to speak in but the arrangement had many advantages as we were able to have actual rostrums to rehearse on and all necessary properties. The war was still in progress and the flying-bomb period had been reached. It was instructive to observe the merest hesitation on the part of the actors as a flying bomb passed over. There was no waiting for the possible cut-out as might have been expected. But all England was behaving in the same way.

Tyrone Guthrie was at his very best in the rehearsals of *Peer Gynt*. He began by showing us all the changes in scenery on a model stage which was an undoubted help to us in such a complicated play.

For *Richard III* there was a screen exhibiting the costumes and a little lecture from Miss Doris Zinkeisen the designer as to how they should be worn. This was certainly instructive, but in actual practice some of

'PEER GYNT', 1944-5
The opening production of the 'new' Old Vic company. Ralph Richardson
appeared in the title role, with Sybil Thorndike as Ase. Richardson was later
awarded the Norwegian medal of St Olav in recognition of his performance.

the dresses were none too easy to get into. To understand the difficulties
that an actor has to wrestle with in his dressing-room requires very
intimate technical knowledge.

The season opened on August 31, 1944 with Guthrie's production of
Peer Gynt in a lively translation by Norman Ginsbury. Old Vic
audiences in the Waterloo Road had a way of giving vociferous
receptions and that first night at the New was no exception. It boded
well for the future of this ambitious enterprise. I played the mad
doctor, Begriffenfeldt, and as he is only on the stage for some fifteen
minutes I was able to watch the play from the front of the house, and I
did this many times. Reece Pemberton's scenery was ingenious and
very successful, and the production was swift in action and simple in
design. It had the rhythm of a dance and moments of great beauty.
I found it entirely satisfying with two exceptions. One was the singing
of the 'Trees'. It was too operatic and vocal. One could hear very
few words and the words in that scene are very important to the final

development of Peer's character. The other was the singing of Solveig's song at the end of the play. Joyce Redman, who suggested very successfully the old woman that Solveig had grown into, could not manage the song and it had to be sung off-stage by a talented member of the Sadler's Wells Opera Company. I think it should have been sung by a diseuse in a thin voice, after the manner of Yvette Guilbert.

Ralph Richardson stretched the wide octave of Peer's life with great skill. He and Sybil Thorndike played the death of Ase superbly. A perfect duet. His old Peer was strange, unearthly and a little terrifying. At first I used to long for something more on those last lines :

> ' *My mother ! My wife ! You holy woman !*
> *Oh, hide me, hide me within your love ! '*

I had a notion that he was holding back the emotion because he was fearful of becoming sentimental, but after he had played the part some time the real feeling came. It was in recognition of his performance of Peer Gynt that King Haakon of Norway presented him with the medal of St Olav.

Laurence Olivier's Button Moulder was utterly different in conception from that of Ion Swinley's and probably was the right one for him to choose. His was a practical, workaday Button Moulder with a forceful personality, and but for the fact that he talked philosophy and moved on silent feet he might have been taken for an ordinary labourer. But with Richardson as his counterpart the scene was gripping and the way the two played together was an object lesson for the young. I am reminded of some words on the art of acting by Harley Granville-Barker. They are from a lecture delivered at Cambridge in 1934 :

> ' Anybody can act. But the highly developed *art* of acting is a very difficult art indeed. It does not consist simply in pretending to be somebody you are not. Nor obviously, can it be *self*-expression, though that is part of the training for it. The definition is inadequate ; but we could call it the expressing of the dramatist's idea in terms of the actor's personality, or the playing of a tune upon the complex and uncertain instrument which is one's physical, emotional and intellectual self. And that is only the beginning of the business. There is the problem of giving to this composite and alien creature, when you have embodied it, adequate expression within the narrow limits of time and opportunity which are all that the longest play and part can afford. There is the still harder problem of reconciling this expression with the equal need for expression of the other characters in the play. *For a good actor is one who not only gives himself utterly to*

LAURENCE OLIVIER AND MARGARET LEIGHTON
As Hotspur and Lady Percy in *Henry IV, Pt I*, 1945-6.

his own part but is responsive enough to his fellows to help them play theirs.
No, it is not an easy art.'

The italics are mine.

Arms and the Man had been given a trial run in Manchester to relieve
the congestion of the rehearsals for three big productions. It was added
to the repertory a few nights after *Peer Gynt* and there was never any
doubt about the success of the Shaw play. War was still in progress
and the author's tilting at the old romantic view of soldiering had an
added sting. Ralph Richardson repeated the rich performance he had
given for me at the Old Vic in 1930 and Laurence Olivier created a
fantastic and extremely funny version of Sergius, and introduced us to
a long line of plastic noses. Sybil Thorndike, Joyce Redman, and

Margaret Leighton added to the laurels they had won in *Peer Gynt*, and Nicholas Hannen's Petkoff was a joy.

The third evening was *Richard III*. It is not Shakespeare at his best, although generations of Saturday night audiences have known it for its stirring melodramatic qualities and have cheered the famous fight to the echo. Shakespeare undoubtedly had a hand in the play and some magnificent pearls of language are strewn, as it were, at the bottom of the sea : but one misses his skill in characterization, and even Richard himself does not really progress. However, the play stands or falls by the king and many great actors have won triumphant success in it. I saw Irving play it ·. . . Richmond had disarmed him and, as he lunged at his breast, Irving caught the sword in his naked hands and through his eyes one felt the sharp edges cutting into the flesh.

Olivier, I believe, knew that he was playing for high stakes when he undertook the part. Since the season in the Waterloo Road under Guthrie he had been absent from the theatre—his Fleet Air Arm service and film work intervening—and he is reported to have said, ' I must make a success '. Well, he certainly did. The long, sharp nose and the lank, black hair tinged with red lying on the shoulders, gave him a satanic appearance that made one give him a wide berth even in the wings.

Certain alterations were made in the text. One I am thankful to say was abandoned before we opened. This was the last scene of *Henry VI*, which was to open the play as a kind of explanatory prologue. I, in the character of Edward IV, had most of the dialogue which I am convinced Shakespeare never wrote, and I hated speaking it. Perhaps the scene was omitted because I did it so badly.

Some lines from one of Gloucester's soliloquies in the same play were, however, very happily incorporated in the well-known opening speech :

> *Now is the winter of our discontent*
> *Made glorious summer by this sun of York.*

None of the critics, by the way, appeared to have noticed these additions. Later in the play one or two scenes were cut, not unwisely perhaps. Herbert Menges composed some excellent incidental music, that written for the appearance of the Ghosts in the tent scene being particularly successful. This, combined with Burrell's stage direction, made that scene more effective than I have ever known it.

I do not think Ralph Richardson ever really enjoyed Richmond. It is a bit of a makeshift, stage-convenience character after all, with not the least resemblance to Henry VII. His uncertainty robbed the fight of some of its excitement. However, Richard's death made up for all. It was a *tour de force*. The frenzied contraction of the limbs which seemed to keep to the rhythm of the music, and, just before his final collapse, the sudden hopeless realization as his eyes look on the cross hilt of his sword that Christ's grace is lost to him for ever, were finely conceived. When the play was given later at the *Comédie Française* the French audience at this point refused to hold themselves in any longer and let loose the whirlwind of their applause. Hard lines on Richmond, who had to finish the play ! Gordon Craig who came to see it in Paris was immensely struck with Laurence Olivier's performance, which, in view of his adoration of his master Henry Irving, was high appreciation. In the Lyceum production Craig had played Edward IV and he did not think much of me in the part, although he was delighted with a soldier

RALPH RICHARDSON
As Falstaff in *Henry IV, Pts I and II*, 1945-6.

I did in the last scenes—a kind of portmanteau role of one-line-gentlemen bundled together and given the name of Captain Blunt. Craig's enthusiasm did not, however, embrace the production work. Indeed, he dismissed it with an expressive but unprintable phrase.

The last play of that season was Chekhov's *Uncle Vanya*. The cast was as follows : Uncle Vanya, Ralph Richardson ; Astrov, Laurence Olivier ; Telyegin, George Relph ; myself as the Professor, Serebryakov ; Marya, Betty Hardy ; Helena, Margaret Leighton ; Sonia, Joyce Redman ; Marina, Sybil Thorndike.

John Burrell was the producer and we started proceedings by sitting round in Sybil Thorndike's dressing-room and reading the play for quite a number of days. For that type of play this is an excellent plan, but I am not sure that we did not go on too long. The other three plays were doing capacity business so there was no great hurry for this fourth production and I think it must have been postponed. I know that I personally was panting to get on to the stage and ' do it in action ' before we came to the end of the readings. I am a slow worker and have to fight through so much before I begin to get at a new part. I find myself in the position of an unborn child—I am a jelly-fish, an animal, a monkey, before I can be born a man—instinctively I go through all my original bad habits—a raw beginner, a bad breather, a user of stage tricks, an actor who over-acts . . . but given time I can shed these pre-natal habits and find something new and better. All producers have their individual methods, and I think it does no harm if they make things a bit difficult for the actor. By that I do not mean bullying the players. That is of no use at all. Burrell's skill needs no advertisement from me. It has been plain to all theatregoers to the New Theatre for the last few years. But there are certainly moments when he made me feel that I was incompetent and ought not to have signed my contract. That state of mind does an actor no harm. Granville-Barker could do the same but in perhaps a more skilful manner. Often when we are bruised and sore and tired that something in the sub-conscious mind manages to struggle out and that is what we have all been looking for !

I have never found a producer to surpass Granville-Barker. He had an intimate knowledge of the play he was working on down to the least significant comma in each part. He never allowed you to slide down the easiest path ; he never gave you intonations and accents but the reason why and where the emphasis should be made.

As I was in *Uncle Vanya* I was not in a position to form any final opinion about the performance as a whole. Intuitively I had a feeling that Richardson should have been cast for Astrov and Olivier for Vanya.

In talks with Richardson I gathered that he thought Uncle Vanya would have been a 'Schopenhauer or a Dostoevsky' if he had been given the chance. I have always thought that whatever opportunities had come his way he would have been a failure, because that is his nature : that is his tragedy.

I saw enough of the play to speak of the exquisite work of George Relph as Telyegin and Sybil Thorndike's solid Russian peasant. Margaret Leighton and Joyce Redman made undoubted successes, and Tanya Moiseiwitsch in designing the scene for the two middle acts created a room that the actors could not help *living* in.

London had now reached the 'rocket' period of the war. At the time it was a saying that one heard the explosion or one was dead. Everyone went about their business seemingly indifferent to the danger of sudden death. A most interesting manifestation of the human spirit.

Earlier in the season arrangements had been made to take the entire company abroad under E.N.S.A. 'lock, stock, and barrel' as the saying is, which meant a skeleton orchestra with conductor (Herbert Menges), scenery, properties, costumes, lighting effects, and staff. When the plan was settled it was expected that the war would still be on, but it came to an end before the conclusion of the season and certain modifications were made. Our tour in the provinces had to be cut to two weeks in Glasgow and two in Manchester.

When this first season closed at the New it had already made an important mark in theatrical history. The two directors who obviously had the best opportunities had achieved high distinction, the company as a whole had created a deep impression and the venture had proved a financial success. So great was the demand for seats that there was a danger of the public becoming tired of trying to get them ! Strangely enough the owner of the New Theatre, Bronson Albery—one of our more catholic-minded theatre managers, and undoubtedly an astute business man—said to me before the season opened, ' I have earned a good deal of money for the Old Vic,' (he was one of the Governors at the time) ' but now they're going to lose it all ! ' It was, it would seem, not one of Mr Albery's best days as a prophet—unless he was looking farther ahead than we can see.

But perhaps the most startling thing about the venture was that the British public (for the first time, I think) had accepted and supported a real repertory of classic plays presented with a constant change of bill. No doubt the public mind had been trained in some measure by the alternating seasons of Old Vic opera and Sadler's Wells ballet at the New, to which I have already referred. It is true that Noel Coward had recently run a successful repertory of his own plays for a limited

'HENRY IV, Pt I', 1945-6
Left to right : David Kentish (Mortimer), George Relph (Worcester), Harcourt Williams (Glendower), Laurence Olivier (Hotspur). Produced by John Burrell ; costumes by Roger Furse, settings by Gower Parks.

season, and Granville-Barker, with Dion Boucicault, had attempted something of the kind at the Duke of York's under Frohman's management with plays by Bernard Shaw, Barrie and Galsworthy. But the success of the first was peculiar to Coward, and the second, owing to the clashing of artistic and commercial interests, was not too successful.

About the visit to Glasgow and Manchester I have nothing to report —except perhaps that I came to appreciate the amazing vitality of Dame Sybil Thorndike. Every day she seemed to be speaking here, giving a recital for some good cause there, attending early service, dealing with correspondence, and acting at night with undiminished vigour. And always in such good spirits and high humour. For myself, I had some glorious walks on the days I was not acting in *Arms and the Man*. Let me advise any actor who has a spare Sunday to go over to Dunoon by the boat and walk via Loch Eck to St Catherine's on Loch Fyne. Twenty miles of beauty and good air and absolute peace in which to think about a new part in particular, or acting in general !

In May the Old Vic Theatre Company embarked at Tilbury for

'THE CRITIC', 1945-6

Left to right : John Garley (Prompter), Laurence Olivier (Mr. Puff), George Relph (Dangle), George Curzon (Sneer). Produced by Miles Malleson ; décor and costumes by Tanya Moiseiwitsch.

Antwerp. We were under E.N.S.A. (the wartime organization headed by Basil Dean for providing entertainment for the Forces), and were all in uniform. We were handed identity discs, and lifebelts with an electric torch attachment. The war was over but a good many enemy submarines were still at large. The ship was crowded with troops and the conditions were very rough and ready. But it did us no harm to experience for a few hours what the rank and file of the Army looked upon as normal. We were not told at the time what our destination was other than ' across the Channel ', and we anchored off Southend until midnight. So with the engines starting up at that time and the Army bread machine cutting bread for the men outside our cabin at four in the morning (we were sixteen to our cabin) there was not much chance of sleep. Orders, too, very soon began to come through the loudspeaker. However, once on the other side, we were driven off to a good breakfast and from that time our life was mostly smooth and comfortable and we were fed in a manner that, at least in Germany, embarrassed some of us.

We played a week at Antwerp and the spacious theatre was packed at every performance by members of the Forces who came in from all quarters. We then went by motor-coach to Brussels. The only available theatre there was too small for us so we went over to Ghent by coach every day—to another fine theatre—and played again to full houses. All through this tour it was always the same, whether it was *Arms and the Man, Richard III* or *Peer Gynt*. The enthusiastic reception of three plays of such varied appeal was illuminating, instructive and very heartening. I used to regret that the local civilian public could not have been allowed to see at least one of the productions, especially in Hamburg. Some of the German actors there were particularly disappointed. But in those early days fraternization was severely forbidden. We flew from Brussels to Hamburg and our theatre was the *Staatliche Schauspielhaus*. The auditorium reminded me of the old Drury Lane that I knew as a child. I think this one was even vaster. We arrived on a Sunday and had plenty of time to crawl all over it. As the curtain was up I climbed to the very back seat in the gallery and got Nicholas Hannen to go to the back of the stage and speak a sentence fairly softly. I heard every word. The last two weeks of this tour were given at the *Comédie Française* under the wing of the British Council and it is no exaggeration to say that the performances took Paris by storm. It was a great experience to act in that historic house. The spirit of Molière haunts the place and one is constantly being reminded of its presence. On entering the stage door the first thing that greets one is a bust of Molière. It is said that for generations the actors, on leaving the theatre after their night's work, have reverently touched the marble with their fingers until, like St Peter's toe in Rome, it bears the indentation of their faith. We ascended either by the stairs, or the very modern and magic lift—a strange but useful anachronism in the midst of ancient tradition, for most of the dressing-rooms are some way from the stage. The lift is built of shining aluminium and has no door. It is guarded merely by a beam of light, and, crossing it, the machinery is set in motion. An affair of witchcraft !

Above stairs is the stately green room—a *Louis Seize* salon. Where are our English green rooms ? Here the walls are crowded with portraits of famous players. The broad corridors are lined with busts of their fellows. The dressing-rooms are for the most part decorated by their present occupiers, one or two a trifle overdone. The one I used, for instance, was like a room in a luxurious Park Lane flat and the screened-off space allotted for make-up was some four feet square.

But it was a charming room with four french windows looking on the *Place de l'Hôtel de Louvre*. On the night of the *Fête Nationale* (July 14) I was able, during my waits, to watch the crowds dancing with unflagging

'RICHARD III', 1944-5
Nicholas Hannen as the Duke of Buckingham, and Laurence Olivier as Richard, in John
Burrell's production.

vitality on the traffic-cleared streets. And not only on that night, but the night before and the night after. Actually the room was ill-adapted for hard work in a theatre. Indeed it was such a showroom that a stream of visitors desired to visit it during the night's work !

The auditorium had an intimate atmosphere. The nearest to it in England is, perhaps, that of the Haymarket. The stage itself was of worn and creaky boards, slit with grooves at the side for the wings— such as the Old Vic had discarded—but sanctified by the tread of great actresses and actors. At the back was an eerie little dark passage that led from one side of the stage to the other. What hands had grasped that guiding rail, tumultuous applause still ringing in the ears, or maybe with the silent dread of failure haunting the heart ? Rachel ? Coquelin ? Sarah ?

What struck me most about the Continental theatres was their spaciousness, not only behind the scenes but also in front of the house. In comparison ours seemed so cheese-paring, niggardly. I sometimes think that we have never recovered from the Puritan crusade of some thirty years against the stage, and the Great British Public still regard the theatre as a sideline of life—a place for lazy relaxation rather than for mental enjoyment or spiritual nourishment. However, now that the Arts Council (late C.E.M.A.) sponsors theatrical enterprise, mostly of the better sort—and in such instances the Entertainment Tax is remitted—theatre work is likely to reach a higher standard and the public taste will rise accordingly. But the public is a fickle jade and the cinema with all its glorious potentialities does not make good theatre audiences.

After a shortened vacation owing to the Paris visit—too short for this kind of company to recuperate in after such a strenuous season, and especially strenuous for the two leading men—we started rehearsals for the second season at the New Theatre.

The programme was to consist of the two parts of *Henry IV*, a double bill including W. B. Yeats's version of *Oedipus* and Sheridan's *The Critic* and occasional performances of *Uncle Vanya*.

The production of a complete *Henry IV* was a noble effort and there can be no question that it was a successful one. I used to think that Baliol Holloway's Falstaff in *The Merry Wives of Windsor* was the best I had seen, but Ralph Richardson's performance was better. One should not really compare the two, however, because the actor who has the opportunity of tackling the character in Parts I and II of *Henry IV* has much better material to work upon than the less witty Falstaff of the Windsor comedy. Richardson has an extraordinary flair for exploiting the humour of actual words, and he introduces no business that is not

'OEDIPUS', 1945-6

Laurence Olivier in the title role, with the Chorus. Produced by Michel Saint-Denis. Décor by John Piper.

germane to the matter. His make-up, as might be expected from one who is skilful with the pencil, was completely conceived, even to the fat gnarled, varicosed legs. He spurned the weakness of those great leather boots in which most Falstaffs hide their spindly legs !

Doll Tearsheet must surely have been born within hearing of Bow Bells but Joyce Redman played her as an Irish trollop, and very effectively. Laurence Olivier was the Hotspur and his bluff humour and virility will be long remembered. He has a gift for arranging realistic stage deaths and Hotspur's end was no exception. Staggered by a blow on the neck from Prince Hal's blade, he stood for some seconds erect on his feet, his hand groping to staunch the blood that oozed through his fingers, and then with startling suddenness plunged in complete armour down a couple of steps on to his face—to be borne off by Falstaff, his body held ignominiously by the heels, dangling down the fat-bellied man's back. On paper one would say an anti-climax, or perhaps a sure laugh— but no, the whole thing held the audience spellbound.

In Part II Olivier played Shallow and I found it difficult to accept his reading. Perhaps I had better confess at once that I had wanted to play the part, in fact at one time it was talked of. Anyway I was physically too big for Shallow. My chief quarrel with Olivier's performance was that he was not of the country, nor indeed were any of his fellows in that Gloucestershire orchard. The Recruits' fun was achieved by means of stage clowning, rather than by virtue of long hours of toil in compelling nature to feed the world, or of sojourning with dumb beasts. It is all a question of points of view and these are raised well enough in the scene between Touchstone and Corin in *As You Like It*. Olivier's comedy, too, arose from business ingenious enough, but having little relation to the dialogue. The delightful humour of Davy pleading for his rascally friend Visor of Wincot just disappeared.

John Burrell produced the two *Henry IV* plays with capital results, and Roger Furse did the costumes. Furse dresses his players in clothes that suit them and look and feel as if they have been lived in. All actors know what joy and comfort that means. Few designers understand as he does what actors have to do in their clothes when it comes to acting.

Oedipus was produced by Michel Saint-Denis. Ever since I saw his work with the *Compagnie de Quinze* at the New Theatre, his direction of Obey's *Noah* when Gielgud played in the English version, and his *Three Sisters*, I have admired his work. Once I had the good fortune to be under his direction in a play called *The Sower of the Hills*. I remember we all worked together for one whole day on a scene which in playing took less than twenty minutes. The play was not perhaps worthy of the work he put into it but the atmosphere he achieved was remarkable and

I came to the conclusion that he was the only producer I had met who could approach Harley Granville-Barker. Of his work on *Oedipus* I am unable to form a judgement as I was only in the opening moments of the play and was always dismissed directly I had done my part. What I did see of the play made me feel that it lacked unity. Yeats's version was not up to his high standard. One felt that he had made it in a hurry to meet some theatre emergency. John Piper's scenery was surrealistic with a very real house portico in the middle of it. I liked the dressing of the chorus and the rhythmical movements that Saint-Denis had devised to the very exciting music of Antony Hopkins. But undoubtedly it was the *tour de force* of Olivier's acting that swept the whole thing to success.

Later in the run I took over the part of Tiresias, the blind prophet, as Ralph Richardson had a film to make and wanted those nights off. The part is entirely a duologue with Oedipus and I enjoyed doing it almost as much as any work that came my way at that time, but I came to the conclusion that I could only act with Olivier when I was blind ! Have I mentioned that critical eye of his ?

Miles Malleson was responsible for *The Critic* and a very good job he made of it. The play was always received uproariously. Olivier's opening scene was a superb piece of comedy and the whole part an example of brilliant virtuosity up to the startling acrobatic feat at the final curtain. One afternoon he nearly took a serious fall. It may be remembered that (in the play) he was accidentally blown sky high— in actual fact into the flies—and descended on the curtain as it swung down. The rope down which he came hand over fist from the flies had inadvertently been taken off its cleat and as he grasped it it came away in his hand. Fortunately his left hand still held the wire that supported the painted cloud he was just leaving and the flymen were able to rescue him from his perilous position. In both plays Olivier's make-up was again remarkable. Without the aid of moustache or beard they seemed so utterly different. It must be admitted that Puff turned up a very intriguing little nose.

As a spectator I sometimes debated what Sheridan really wanted of his actors in this play within a play. Are they good actors performing bad stuff and burlesquing it, or are they bad actors being unconsciously funny in Puff's rodomontade play ? Whichever was intended, I thought Joyce Redman overdid her mimicry of Tilburina and at times made it very uphill work for the actress who played that part. But she kept the audience in fits of laughter.

Towards the end of the season a lightning visit to New York was planned. As I am a good sailor and adore a sea voyage the prospect

HERBERT MENGES
Director of Music to the Old Vic Theatre Company since 1934.

delighted me. Then it was decided to send the scenery by sea and fly the company. Well, I don't enjoy flying so I decided not to go, which unfortunately put a good deal of work on all sorts of people re-rehearsing my parts. That the visit was an outstanding success must still be remembered—although Bernard Shaw asserts that a fortnight is the limit of the public's memory. The company had a rollicking good time and it was without doubt a grand thing to do not only for the Old Vic itself but for the prestige of the British Theatre.

After the last night of this, the second season at the New, I left the company. I was disappointed in a way that there seemed to be nothing for me in the future work, but I knew that at my time of life two years was quite long enough to be part of any organization. Laurence Olivier, in his last-night speech, made extremely endearing references to my coming departure and bade me a public farewell, all of which I found extremely moving.

XVIII

The Gods Depart

THE coming season was to herald changes and a shift in policy. Olivier was to appear only in the part of Lear and not beyond Christmas. Ralph Richardson was scheduled for the part of Cyrano de Bergerac. Ben Jonson's *The Alchemist* and a new Priestley play were also to be done. Lear proved an unexampled success and was sold out for all performances. Bronson Albery said the advance booking was phenomenal, only to be compared with successful pantomimes ! About its artistic success the public were almost unanimous. Some found that the play did not move them emotionally, but one often finds with great tragedies such as *Lear*, *Macbeth*, and *Hamlet* that such deep impressions are made on people's minds that they cannot bring an unbiased judgement to bear on any new point of view. Taken as a whole, I thought it was a fine production and for the most part finely played.

For the contraries, two rather heavy house pieces left and right of the stage were mounted on trucks—that is, low platforms fitted with small wheels—and became a little tiresome as they were frequently moved into place and away again. Even Herbert Menges's excellent incidental music failed to cover the noise. I thought the ingenuousness of Gloucester's journey from his castle to the hovel defeated its own end because it distracted the attention from the important matter in hand. Also, the dramatic meeting between the disguised Edgar and his father entirely misfired. The gay colouring of Roger Furse's décor was an admirable setting for the tragedy—the antithesis of blue skies to a Greek tragedy. For the acting, much of Olivier's Lear was magnificent both in conception and execution. Margaret Leighton's reading of Goneril as a luxurious, over-sexed creature came off and made a good contrast to Pamela Brown's Regan. This was most refreshing, as actresses taking these two parts so often play the same game. That good actor George Relph got every ounce out of Gloucester. But the performance that will

LAURENCE OLIVIER
As Lear, in his own production of 1946-7.

live longest in the memory, I believe, is Alec Guinness's Fool.   It was an
epitome of all the wisdom in the world falling in stray shreds from a
clown's chalked face.   It had the beady eyes, the questioning eyebrows,
the comedy and pathetic inability to cope with life that was once Grock's.
It had that strangeness too, which, Bacon tells us, is to be found in all
excellent beauty.

Lear is a play of granite.   One cannot expect to find it chiselled into
a complete statue.   But it must be attempted over and over again.   I
have seen four Lears : Benson, Gielgud, Wolfit, Olivier.   Each of these
actors brought deep insight and technical ability to bear on the part.
Without attaching any value to my opinion, which is here obviously
laid open to the charge of prejudice, I thought Gielgud in his original
portrayal of the part at the Old Vic in 1930 the nearest to the titanic
figure.   Gordon Bottomley in a letter to Gielgud wrote : ' I cannot
believe that I shall ever see it more worthily done.   People used to say
" Lear is for the study ".   What nonsense !   It only comes to its
completest life on the stage . . . I cannot believe that either you or
anyone else can ever be (or can ever have been) more convincingly
Lear than you were last night.'

How well I remember the thrill of his first entrance—stepping
majestically down a steep slope between a forest of tall, scarlet spears to
music so successfully composed by Herbert Menges ; and that odd twist
to the neck, as if the head were too heavy for it, which gave at once a
sense of mental danger.

The new Priestley play, *An Inspector Calls*, was produced on October 1,
1946.   It did not attract such large audiences as other plays in the
repertory.   One wonders why ?   The story was an intriguing one and
told with the same ingenuity that the author had employed in his earlier
play *Dangerous Corner*.   It was perfectly cast and directed by Basil Dean
on the top of his form.   Possibly it may have wrung our withers too
particularly ; very few of us could escape the author's implied
condemnation, not if we had a grain of honesty about us.   Or perhaps it
required too much concentration on the part of the audience.   ' Theatregoers in London ', said Hugh Walpole, ' are almost without exception
bored if they are asked to do any thinking.'   It may well be that the
audiences that thronged to *Richard III*, *Peer Gynt*, and the *Henry* plays
wanted colour, costume, romance, something they could love, the drama
of an earlier age, and were not interested in a modern problem.   Truly
the mentality of the public is an enigma.   I wish it could be induced
to accept a greater responsibility for the theatre.

Cyrano de Bergerac appeared on October 24.   Can Rostand's play be
successfully achieved in the English language ?   The verse depends so

ALEC GUINNESS
As the Fool, in *King Lear*, 1946-7.

greatly on the original metre, on subtle nuances, and often on rhyming jokes—of which many have no counterpart in our idiom. The version used at the New was little better than most and suffered as well some grievous cuts.

Ralph Richardson has the qualifications for a first-rate Cyrano. In many ways his technique is akin to that of the Latin actors (which often puzzles the British onlooker) ; but here he was crippled by the pedestrian dialogue and Guthrie's not too happy production. Tyrone Guthrie can do such beautiful work and yet, at times, he seems to say, ' This is extravagance, let's have a joke ! ' I did not find the death of Cyrano happily devised. His utter unselfishness, his courage, and over all still his panache, were blurred by a trick plunge forward into the arms of the two figures who caught him, figures which successfully fogged the climax.

Ben Jonson's play *The Alchemist* was one of Burrell's most happy productions. The date was January 15, 1947. The whole company

GEORGE RELPH
In the title role of *The Alchemist*, 1946-7.

was on its toes, working well together, but in a shining Milky Way of good acting George Relph's glorious Alchemist must be accorded Alpha brilliance.

Oddly enough, before the curtain rang up on the first night the company were in the depths of despondency. Legend says that when John Burrell called the company in the morning and said that they would just run through the words, George Relph retorted : ' That's the one thing we can't do. We don't know them ! ' However, the opening night was received with roars of approval (Old Vic, Waterloo Road vintage). Alec Guinness as Abel Drugger won a special acclamation when he spoke his line, ' Have you ever seen me play the fool ? '

The Alchemist drew full houses even through the snow and ice of the spring of 1947, when the rehearsals for *Richard II* had temporarily to be abandoned because there was neither light to read by, nor heat to keep the players warm.

Alec Guinness as the King, in keeping with all his work which is always exquisite, gave an unusual and, in some ways remarkable, performance. His face was like a book. He has a rare facility for altering the quality of his appearance without, I should say, the aid of make-up. It must be done by the muscles in his face. One dreads to take one's eyes from his face even when he is not speaking for fear of missing some flitting shade of thought.

Ralph Richardson's production was picturesque and lively in Michael Warre's ingenious setting. It allowed the play to move forward with Elizabethan swiftness. The tall, slender, ' Perpendicular ' pillars grouped in the centre satisfied the imagination by seeming to be trees in the garden scene and later prison bars hemming in the unhappy King. There were, however, some lamentable cuts in the text, notably the Queen's first scene. This reduced her part, which is not a great one, to that of a nonentity. It robbed the Duke of York (played admirably by Lewis Casson) of a characteristic outburst, and made hash of those caterpillars of the commonwealth, Bushy, Bagot and Green, and their relations to the characters of Richard and Bolingbroke. Finally it had the effect of shortening the King's Irish expedition to the point of absurdity and detracted from the drama of his return. The production lacked poetry and, occasionally, glamour. One sensed a strain to evade the emotion of the play. Perhaps there was an unconscious determination to forget past successes. The scene in Westminster Hall failed to make its full effect. Richard's dress gave him little help. Royalty usually manages to look its best in any circumstances. Charles I managed it at his trial and Marie Antoinette, though very simply dressed at hers, looked superb. For some reason the King's last words and rapid exit lacked personal dignity, but Guinness played the prison scene superbly, although the producer robbed him of the full effect of the music. It should be played off-stage by a wandering musician on a pipe or a hurdy-gurdy. My own reaction to the groom was that if he had as little feeling as he was allowed to show—why did he bother to see the King at all, which can have been no easy matter ?

In January 1947, before the close of the season and during the ' ice age ' of those early months of the year, the formal opening of the Old Vic School took place on the stage of the old theatre which, through the sympathetic influence of Ellen Wilkinson, had so far had its war damage repaired that it was now able to house the school. But the front of the house had not been touched as yet and for some of us who had known the theatre so intimately it was rather a painful experience to pick one's way across the floor denuded of seats and stacked with dusty bits of scenery and broken properties. It was sad to see the decoration hanging like tattered flags from the ceiling, and the famous Lilian Baylis box a deserted cavern with the red curtain flapping in the breeze. On the stage, however, all was clean and bright, and a goodly company assembled. The only warmth seemed to come from an oil stove in what had been the prompt corner and where in ancient days Lilian Baylis had cooked her chops on the gas ring. The cold was intense, but hearts were warm and those who spoke—Lord Lytton and Ellen Wilkinson, both now lost to us—spoke well. Laurence Olivier also made a short speech, and as it was addressed particularly to the students and is on the subject of acting, I have asked him to allow me to quote from it :

' The growth of your career should be like that of a tree, a simple, steady, all-round growth. You are now about, I hope, to sink your roots deep into the fertile ground of this institution, in order to assure yourselves of as strong a stem as possible, so that however gloriously your branches may flourish they shall not want for resourcefulness and poise. There is plenty of wind, torrents of rain, and no end of thunder about, so don't get too tall too quickly. There is no more invidious state in a career, than that in which one finds one's reputation out-growing one's experience.

' All I ask, as an audience, is to believe what I see and hear. An actor, above all, must be the great understander, either by intuition, observation or both, and that puts him on the level with a doctor, a priest or a philosopher. If I can get more from him than just belief, then I feel both fortunate and overjoyed . . . there are many dimensions in the art of acting, but NONE of them . . . are good or interesting . . . unless they are invested with the appearance, or complete illusion of truth. The difference between the actual truth and the illusion of the truth is what you are about to learn. You will not finish learning it until you are dead.'

And in connection with that last truism he told a story of Henry Irving. Towards the end of that great actor's life he had a serious illness from which he recovered enough to continue acting until his death. During the illness he had a conversation with his friend and manager Bram Stoker. ' I think this may be the end,' he said. ' It does seem a pity to go now that I am beginning to find out something about acting.'

So the third season at the New Theatre drew to a close. It had been slightly less successful financially than the first two and it is too early to diagnose the cause. The exceptionally hard winter and the drastic fuel restrictions proved very bad for all entertainment business and the slowing down of spending power was already beginning. The temporary departure of Laurence Olivier after Christmas, so that he might be free

OLD VIC THEATRE SCHOOL

Students at rehearsal on the stage of the Old Vic. Wartime bomb damage closed the famous old building in the Waterloo Road to the public : but it was reopened in January 1947 to house the school. The wicker cages in the top left-hand corner of the picture were built for the ' madhouse ' scene in Guthrie's production, in 1944, of *Peer Gynt*.

202

to make the film of *Hamlet*, was bound to affect a proportion of the Old Vic public, although in ideal conditions this should not be. An audience that thinks in terms of plays and not of favourite stars should support an organization doing such first-class work as the Old Vic had been doing at the New for three years, without clamouring for this or that personality. But for that to happen in this country I fear we must have not only a school for actors but one for audiences. Among the many things that they would have to learn would be manners in a playhouse, and how to wrestle with their amazing phobia that they cannot sit through two hours of entertainment without eating and drinking. I am sure the simple-minded would be most surprised to learn that cellophane and chocolate wrappings not only disturb their neighbours but can utterly discomfort a poor actor who is carrying on his extremely nervous occupation of juggling with his emotions and concentrating his thoughts for their diversion.

To the delight of his many admirers and his own colleagues the honour of knighthood was bestowed upon Ralph Richardson for services rendered to the Theatre. At the time I was continually asked why the honour had been given to Richardson and not to Olivier, so I invented an explanation which, of course, had not a grain of truth in it. I said that the Prime Minister wanted to honour the Old Vic Theatre Company but did not know which partner to choose, so Olivier and Richardson tossed up for it and Richardson called heads and won. But the inclusion of Sir Laurence Olivier's name in the Birthday Honours list a few months later poured oil on troubled waters of admiration. The important point about the whole matter is that the honours were given for services rendered to the Theatre, and to the Old Vic in particular. I imagine also that Olivier's honour was due partly to his brilliant direction of the *Henry V* film which must have greatly added to the prestige of British art all the world over.

Looking back for a moment over the three years at the New Theatre, even the most captious critic must admit that in the history of the English Theatre the seasons under Richardson, Olivier, and Burrell will take a very important place. I who knew the Old Vic of Lilian Baylis's day cannot pretend that it is the same. It is not : but life changes from hour to hour ; how can the theatre escape the inevitable ? Three men of cultural integrity and unquestioned ability in the art of the theatre gathered up the threads of the original organization which the black hurricane of war had blown hither and thither, and wove them into a pattern again, but a slightly different pattern. It was an undertaking that required great courage, foresight and patience. I sometimes think that it could never have been done but for the old friendship that existed between Richardson and Olivier.

GLEN BYAM SHAW, MICHEL SAINT-DENIS AND GEORGE DEVINE
The directors of the Old Vic Theatre Centre meet at a rehearsal break. In the
background are students of the Old Vic Theatre School.

That great comedian Charles Hawtrey once said, ' I would rather have a not-so-good actor than a difficult one.' As conceit, ill-temper, and selfishness sow seeds of spiritual disquiet that can wreck the best company of players, so simplicity, understanding, and consideration are even more powerful in their affirmative quality. While I was with the company at the New there was a charming little ritual carried out probably as a joke. At the end of the play when the whole company had taken a number of calls, whoever was playing the leading part would take a curtain call. If it was Richardson, Olivier would hold back the curtain for him, and when it was Olivier's turn, Richardson would perform the like office for him. This little courtesy is usually undertaken by the stage manager. A matter of no great importance, perhaps, but significant.

XIX

'Other Knee, Sonnie'

I AM not one of those who can see good only in the past, but I venture to assert that a sound performance of Shakespeare cannot be given without keeping to some of the rules. The poet's original conception must be appreciated and the contemporary values of his time considered. He wrote his plays in verse because he intended his dialogue to make an emotional as well as a dramatic effect, and, although it is sometimes necessary to help our modern audiences by illuminating the text with intelligent emphasis, it is neither right nor expedient to speak the verse as prose. Once when one of my company was losing the musical rhythm of the verse Granville-Barker said to me, ' Don't let your actors be so damned explanatory ! ' Listening to the play of *Coriolanus* at the New Theatre in the spring of 1948 I often found it difficult to remember that it was a poetic drama.

The pushing of Elizabethan plays back into the picture-frame theatre is bound to make difficulties for the producer, and I doubt if Mrs Siddons herself could have spoken successfully those five lines of welcome to Coriolanus as Rosalind Atkinson was asked to say them. They were written for declamation on the platform stage, not to be spoken into the wings. As Volumnia Miss Atkinson, a versatile actress of distinction, gave an extremely interesting performance and expressed a lovableness in the character which is rare. One regretted that one of her best scenes, that in which she turns on the Tribunes, was blue-pencilled. Why I cannot imagine.

John Clements carried the difficult part of Coriolanus with style and vigour, and he and Harry Andrews played their strange duet of hate and admiration with spirit. Alec Guinness deservedly won rich praise for his Menenius, but I am beginning to wonder if this fine actor is not carrying an intellectual approach to his work farther than is wise. In this reaction from over-emphasis and false sentiment he exhibits a cold

'CORIOLANUS', 1947-8

John Clements in the title role, with Rosalind Atkinson as Volumnia. Produced by
E. Martin Browne.

reserve which seems to prevent a scene from catching fire. Though
to tell the truth he had little encouragement to incendiarism in the scene
with the Volscian guards.   The two moments in the play that moved me
—and one must be moved in the theatre—were the almost silent meeting
of Coriolanus and his wife, and, in quite a different way, the three-
handed scene between the Volscian servants discussing Coriolanus
after Aufidius had accepted him as a friend and ally. This little scene
was played with perfect balance by George Rose, John Garley, and Frank
Duncan, and what was particularly heartening was the fact that one of
them had been a humble ranker in the original 1944 season, and the
other two since 1945. They displayed the essence of team work and the
kind of growth that a first-rate repertory company should aim at.

The décor of this play was simple but not very imaginative, and the
two dominant columns seemed to lack nothing but the smoke from the
factory chimneys.

If the token crowd of plebeians had been individually alive it would
have passed muster, but the paucity of patricians and senators was surprising and damaging to the balance of the play's dramatic conflict.

'RICHARD II', 1946-7
Left to right : Margaret Leighton (Queen), Ralph Richardson (Gaunt), Alec
Guinness (Richard). Produced by Ralph Richardson.

Judged by the exceedingly high standard set by the New Theatre seasons
at their best the production was not up to par. It lacked backbone;
but the play came out well enough, and those members of the public
who did not trouble to see it are not to be congratulated. James Agate
(in the columns of the *Sunday Times*) once told a lady who had complained
that a play had been withdrawn before she could get to see it, ' Madam,
one day you will wake up to find that there is no theatre ! '

I have purposely dealt with the last production of this season first
because it was the only important Shakespearean one. *Richard II* had
already been presented at the end of the previous season. Before coming
to London the company had taken part in the Edinburgh Festival and
subsequently visited one or two other towns.

The Old Vic organization has been criticized for its Metropolitanism,
but besides the extensive wartime touring activities, a branch of the
Old Vic has been doing well-chosen work at Bristol in that exquisite
old playhouse the Theatre Royal, and the Young Vic has toured plays
for the entertainment of audiences-to-be, notably *King Stag*, *The Snow
Queen*, and *The Knight of the Burning Pestle*. Then there was the rocket-

GEORGE RELPH AS GRUMIO   PETER COPLEY AS TRANIO
In *The Taming of the Shrew*, 1947-8.

propelled visit to New York in 1941, and, finally, the Old Vic Australian
tour headed by Laurence Olivier, Vivien Leigh, and George Relph in
1948.

When the 1947-8 season opened at the New, I was acting in *You Never
Can Tell* across the way and so was unable to see the early productions.
I did, however, manage to get a glimpse of *The Taming of the Shrew* and
Gogol's *The Government Inspector*, as the management kindly arranged for
me to stand dressed as William the Waiter at the back of a box.

The Taming of the Shrew promised to be a gay production influenced,
I imagine, by the *Commedia del Arte*, but carried out with financial
resources that were beyond my reach when I attempted it in 1932.
Trevor Howard was a colourful Petruchio with a beard straight out of
an early Millais before he began painting pot-boilers. I thought
Howard and Patricia Burke carried off the first wooing scene with gusto
and skill. Other notable performances were Peter Copley's ingenious
Tranio and George Relph's Grumio.

I was not a little puzzled by the superstructure on the left of the stage
upon which Sly retired to bed. The puzzle probably resolved itself
later in the play, but up to the moment of my leaving my box it suggested
some giant's billiard table.

Of *The Government Inspector* I saw even less. It started off with tremendous verve and was picturesquely comic. Whether it was over-caricatured, as some said, I am not in a position to judge, but certainly the fantasticos of the first act did not tell me a clear story. Unfortunately I saw no more of Alec Guinness than his exquisite entrance.

What a magnificent play *St Joan* is ! It has some of the universal appeal of *Hamlet*. The ' west wind ' scene moved me as much as ever, and I think I have never seen the tent scene played as well. Celia Johnson is a fine actress and her Joan was a fine achievement. She made one see the woman and not the actress. Her only shortcoming was the outburst at the end of the trial scene. Whether she had not the reserve for that torrent of indignation and pent-up emotion, or whether her career has not forced her to develop the muscles that give an actor the power of sustained deep breathing, I cannot say. The spiritual quality of her reading was never in doubt. Alec Guinness presented an intriguing Dauphin. The physical awkwardness of those hanging hands held in a slightly abnormal position, and the lack-lustre eye, reflected the numbness of the mind. Looking back on the performance it appears a little static. It is not necessary to compare two such opposite conceptions as his and Ernest Thesiger's in the original production,

' THE TAMING OF THE SHREW ', 1947-8
Produced by John Burrell. Centre : Grumio (George Relph), watches Petruchio (Trevor Howard) carry off Katharina (Patricia Burke).

'THE GOVERNMENT INSPECTOR', 1947-8
Gogol's comedy was produced by John Burrell, with décor by Feliks Topolski. Left to right : Rosalind Atkinson (Anna), Bernard Miles (Dmukhanovsky), Alec Guinness (Khlestakov), Harry Andrews (Osip), Renée Asherson (Marya).

but the latter's curious, rebellious crackle of wit lit up the ineffectual creature ; leavened the dough of his weakness. Mark Dignam was the Cauchon and Harry Andrews the best Warwick I have seen. It was these two players, of course, who handled the tent scene so brilliantly.

The play was taken at a good pace. Without casting any slur on Frank Duncan, I wonder why the management, who could produce an excellent imp for Falstaff's page, were unable to do the like for the Kingfisher's speech ? Only a boy can speak those lines. Something must have gone wrong with Joan's recognition of the Dauphin the afternoon I was present. The effect admirably planned by the author did not come off.

Weighing up my impressions of this season as a whole I am inclined to agree with the point of view expressed by T. C. Worsley in the *New Statesman*—that it is not good enough. When, in June 1948, I saw the Liverpool Repertory Company at the St James's in *The Cherry Orchard* I could not help drawing comparisons. One cannot judge a repertory company on one performance, but this was first-rate both in individual characterization and team work. Gladys Boot in particular, though not a perfect type for the part, gave a lovely performance. What a misfortune it was for the theatre that Ellen Terry never played Madame Ranevsky !

Last season's coming and going of the leading players was probably the cause of the lack of cohesion. The solidarity of the company from the rise of the curtain on the opening play until its fall at the end of the season used to be the firm policy of the Old Vic, and the sooner we return to it the better.

At the end of his article in the *New Statesman* Mr Worsley writes :

' There has been a lack of a real " conception " behind the productions as if no one has had time to think them out properly in the first place. They have to be got on and they are got on— somehow. The labour of administration and organization are probably immense and anyone who knew the difficulties under which Mr John Burrell and his company work would probably sympathize. But that is not the point. The point is that in its first fine flight the new Old Vic was hailed as a glorious fresh start and the reputation acquired has given it a stamp which its performances no longer justify. . . . If it could retire to its proper place across the river charging popular prices and being what it used to be, criticism would be less exacting. But so long as it aims at being a national theatre, it is the unpleasant duty of the critic to repeat : This is simply not good enough.'

And talking of a national theatre, one must not forget the work at Stratford-on-Avon where, in the year of grace 1948, Sir Barry Jackson set up a standard of work which cannot be ignored.

'ST JOAN', 1947-8

Celia Johnson played the title role in John Burrell's production of Shaw's play. Left to right : Kenneth Edwards (Archbishop), Cecil Winter (La Hire), Alec Guinness (Dauphin).

XX

All's Well

ALL'S WELL. No, that does not stand for an abbreviation of one of Shakespeare's less popular plays, but for the cry of the lookout man from the crow's nest of a ship at sea. All is well if we will but have the courage to demonstrate our faith by giving proof of it in the fuller development of the life about us. So what of the future?

When I began this book there was talk of an amalgamation between the National Theatre and the Old Vic. One heard of a building not far from Waterloo Bridge on the proposed new embankment south of the Thames. Now the Government are to take a hand, and, although we shall still have to wait for our National Theatre, it has suddenly become a definite proposition.

I have been reading Harley Granville-Barker's second book on the subject, published privately in 1930, and I hope that the wisdom of that prophet of the theatre will be listened to with understanding. It is not within the scope of this book to go into details of such an enterprise, but let us hope that the building will be spacious enough in every particular—not forgetting the amenities to be enjoyed by the actors and the staff who will have the work to do. And let us beware of those who have not worked in a theatre putting a finger in the pie. When I say 'worked in a theatre' I mean such a grounding as Gordon Craig would call work.

I am one of those who hold the opinion that the training of a company should have begun long ago for this purpose of a National Theatre, and must certainly be begun before the first brick is laid. In some degree the Old Vic has such a company already in being, but it would need to be developed on a more generous scale than its present constitution allows, and as the building that is to house the National Theatre cannot be completed for some years, now is the time to take the matter in hand.

The question of a Director is going to be a vexed one. Should a man or a woman occupy the post ?   With a cloud of witnesses—from Queen Elizabeth to Queen Victoria and Florence Nightingale, and in our own times, from cabinet ministers to Lilian Baylis and Ninette de Valois— it would be absurd to rule a woman out if she were the right person. The first Director should be in the prime of life, having had sound experience as a worker in the theatre which should definitely include acting and producing.   He would, of course, have producers under him, but should also produce occasionally himself.   He should be a man of culture, and besides being a skilled organizer, should also be a philosopher and a humane man, but yet one possessing the hardness and flexibility of steel.   In short a genius !

What troubles me most about the National Theatre is the attitude of the public.   How are we to become theatre-minded ?   We have little claim to such a title at the moment.   How can we all be induced to accept our share of responsibility ?

When the population was smaller and theatre going more concentrated the interest in it was more intense as we can learn from such critics as Hazlitt, Lamb, and Leigh Hunt.   Granville-Barker wrote, 'Kean's audiences at Drury Lane were not of the indifferent, acquiescent, " amuse-me-if-you-can " temper of theatre audiences today, but liker by far to the crowd in the centre court at Wimbledon when the finals are being played.   They knew a masterly stroke when they saw one.'

The task before us is to persuade the public that plays and the art of acting are more important than individual stars.   The National Theatre would be doomed to failure if it pursued a policy of importing stars. It is the business of a first-rate theatre to make not stars but great actors. More than once I have known fine work done in a theatre associated with famous names—work which attracted a wide public ; yet when the ' names ' were withdrawn the attendances began to decline, although the actual work of the company as a whole was *just as good*.

Can one say too often that the living theatre is a trinity of actors, playwrights, and auditors ?   To call forth fine plays and great acting the audience must give as generously as do the players and the play.   It is only when this miracle is achieved that the best authors are encouraged to write for the theatre as was proved in the historic Court Theatre season, 1904-7.

I once saw a Chinese play that began with an act of worship. Religion need not mean solemn ritual : we need farce as well as tragedy. But reverence is not an undesirable attitude of mind.   The Puritan ban still hangs about the conscience of the playgoer as a kind of inherited tradition.   Was it not Shaw who said that there are still those who believe in the omnipresence of God—except in the theatre ?

Can the Press help us in the education of the theatregoer? Editors could, I believe, play a valiant part. We have a nucleus of dramatic critics. Is there any reason why that nucleus should not be enlarged? If space is a difficulty, most of us would gladly sacrifice the gossip columns —the National Theatre would not need such ' puffs '—so that the space saved might be devoted to our real work. The commercial theatre has undoubtedly induced us all to sacrifice much dignity and not a little illusion, and to create a journalistic view of us which has often been our own downfall.

And what of the original Old Vic building in the Waterloo Road? Architecturally it is not uncomely. There is a pleasing solidity about it and a simplicity of line that sorts well with modern standards. The theatre itself is a practicable workshop and has many advantages over the cramped space of most West End theatres. It would be a thousand pities if we lost it.

The conception of a popular theatre inaugurated by Emma Cons and developed by Lilian Baylis must not be entirely overlooked. While admitting that the original purpose may have passed away owing to the variation in values during the last fifty years, I do not think that Lilian Baylis would have willingly sanctioned the high-priced seats recently necessitated by the unavoidable commitments of a West End theatre—except possibly as a temporary measure. This, of course, is no criticism of Bronson Albery whose approach to the Old Vic has ever been generous and helpful. The 'Regulars', as the old following of the theatre are called, naturally feel that they have been elbowed out of an institution for whose creation they were partly responsible. But it cannot be expected that conditions appertaining to the opening of the century can be maintained when two unprecedented wars have shaken our civilization to its foundations.

Ellen Terry once expressed the opinion that in many ways art institutions outlived their usefulness in twenty-five years. She may have been thinking of the Lyceum under Henry Irving. The truth in that idea may be applicable to the Old Vic, but there is no reason why it should not be reconstituted—as indeed it has been twice already, and at intervals of roughly a quarter of a century : once in 1914 and again in 1944.

We, who knew Lilian Baylis intimately, believe that had she been alive she would have persuaded (or coerced !) the authorities to let her patch up the war-wounded building and reopen it to her dear public. In many ways I think this a circumstance devoutly to have been wished. I imagine that those now in command of the ship have no great liking for a return to the Lower Marsh. If that is so, it is to be wished, also devoutly, that any such personal disinclination will not blur their vision when considering the needs of those who have ever been the real lovers of the theatre. I am thinking of those ideal lovers, not of the Old Vic in particular, but of that universal theatre which is one of those things we humans need other than our daily bread.

Appendix A
OLD VIC PLAYS AND THEIR PRODUCERS

THIS list gives the plays produced by Old Vic companies at the Old Vic theatre from 1914 to 1940, and at the New Theatre from 1944 to 1949. Plays produced in London from 1941 to 1944 are also included.

1914-15

The Merchant of Venice
The Tempest
The Merry Wives of
     Windsor
The Taming of the Shrew
King Rene's Daughter
The Comedy of Errors
Twelfth Night
A Midsummer Night's Dream
She Stoops to Conquer
As You Like It
The Winter's Tale
The School for Scandal
Othello
Hamlet
Macbeth
Julius Caesar

Producers : MATHESON LANG and HUTIN BRITTON (*The Merchant of Venice, The Taming of the Shrew, Hamlet*) ; BEN GREET (*The Tempest, King Rene's Daughter, The Comedy of Errors, A Midsummer Night's Dream, The Winter's Tale, Othello, Macbeth*) ; ANDREW LEIGH (*Twelfth Night, As You Like It,* and—with ESTELLE STEAD—*The Merry Wives of Windsor*) ; LADY BENSON (*She Stoops to Conquer*) ; MRS EDWARD COMPTON (*The School for Scandal*) ; J. FISHER WHITE (*Julius Caesar*).

1915-16

As You Like it
The Merchant of Venice
Henry V
The Rivals

The Tempest
Othello
Richard III
A Midsummer Night's Dream
Julius Caesar
The Winter's Tale
She Stoops to Conquer
The Star of Bethlehem
Romeo and Juliet
Hamlet
Much Ado About Nothing
Macbeth
The Taming of the Shrew
Twelfth Night
Everyman
The School for Scandal

Producer : BEN GREET

1916-17

The School for Scandal
The Rivals
Henry VIII
The Comedy of Errors
As You Like It
The Merchant of Venice
Julius Caesar
The Tempest
Othello
Richard II
The Two Gentlemen of
     Verona
King Rene's Daughter
She Stoops to Conquer
The Star of Bethlehem
A Christmas Carol
Twelfth Night
The Taming of the Shrew
Macbeth
Everyman
Henry V

St Patrick's Day
The Critic
Much Ado About Nothing
The Lady of Lyons
The Merry Wives of
     Windsor
Hamlet

Producer : BEN GREET

1917-18

King John
The Merchant of Venice
Richard II
As You Like It
Henry IV, Pt II
Julius Caesar
The Tempest
The Taming of the Shrew
A Christmas Carol
Seaman's Pie
The Star of Bethlehem
The School for Scandal
She Stoops to Conquer
A Midsummer Night's Dream
The Winter's Tale
Romeo and Juliet
King Lear
Cymbeline
Henry VIII
The Merry Wives of
     Windsor
Henry V
Twelfth Night
Everyman
Richard III
Masks and Faces
Hamlet

Producer : BEN GREET

217

1918-19

The Merchant of Venice
Hamlet
Measure for Measure
Much Ado About Nothing
Macbeth
Twelfth Night
The Tempest
Henry V
As You Like It
Love's Labour's Lost
The Coventry Nativity Play
The Taming of the Shrew
A Midsummer Night's Dream
The Winter's Tale
Julius Caesar
Everyman
Henry IV, Pt I

Producers : G. R. Foss, all plays with the exceptions of The Coventry Nativity Play, Patrick Kirwan ; Everyman, Ben Greet.

1919-20

The Merry Wives of
               Windsor
The Tempest
Richard II
As You Like It
Henry V
Macbeth
She Stoops to Conquer
The Hope of the World
A Christmas Carol
The Taming of the Shrew
The Merchant of Venice
Julius Caesar
A Midsummer Night's Dream
Hamlet
Everyman
The Rivals
Othello
Coriolanus
Henry IV, Pts I and II
The Land of Heart's Desire
The Proposal
Michael
Gallant Cassian

Producers : Russell Thorndike and Charles Warburton, all plays with the exceptions of The Land of

Heart's Desire, Betty Potter ; The Proposal, Stockwell Hawkins ; Gallant Cassian, Ernest Milton. The producer of Michael is not recorded.

Costumes and settings for all productions by Wilfrid Walter.

1920-1

The Winter's Tale
The School for Scandal
As You Like It
Twelfth Night
King John
The Taming of the Shrew
The Hope of the World
The Comedy of Errors
Pantaloon
The Merchant of Venice
Julius Caesar
A Midsummer Night's Dream
Romeo and Juliet
Everyman
The Tempest
Hamlet
Richard III
Warrior's Day
King Lear
Pericles

Producer : Robert Atkins

Costumes for The School for Scandal by Tom Heslewood ; for all other productions by Neil Curtis. Settings for all productions by Wilfrid Walter.

1921-2

Much Ado About Nothing
Richard II
As You Like It
Macbeth
Henry V
Wat Tyler
All's Well That Ends Well
Advent
The Merchant of Venice
Othello
Twelfth Night
Peer Gynt
King Lear
Everyman

Love Is the Best Doctor
The Comedy of Errors
Hamlet
Timon of Athens
She Stoops to Conquer
Vic Vicissitudes

Producers : Robert Atkins, all plays with the exception of She Stoops to Conquer, Rupert Harvey.

Costumes for Richard II, Macbeth, and Wat Tyler by John Garside. Settings for Macbeth and Peer Gynt by Robert Atkins ; for all other productions by Wilfrid Walter.

1922-3

The Merry Wives of
               Windsor
The Taming of the Shrew
Henry IV, Pts I and II
Julius Caesar
A New Way to Pay
              Old Debts
Britain's Daughter
Antony and Cleopatra
The Hope of the World
The Cricket on the Hearth
The Merchant of Venice
Henry VI, Pts I, II and III
Richard III
King Arthur
Everyman
Twelfth Night
Hamlet
A Midsummer Night's Dream

Producer : Robert Atkins

Costumes and settings for all productions by Hubert Hine.

1923-4

Love's Labour's Lost
Titus Andronicus
Henry V
Troilus and Cressida
The Two Gentlemen of
              Verona
As You Like It
The Play of the Shepherds
A Christmas Carol
The School for Scandal

Henry VIII
The Tempest
Faust
The Rivals
Coriolanus
The Merchant of Venice
Everyman
Hamlet
Twelfth Night

Producer : ROBERT ATKINS
Costumes for all productions
by TOM HESLEWOOD ; settings
by HUBERT HINE.

1924-5

Othello
A Midsummer Night's Dream
Hannele
The Play of the Shepherds
She Stoops to Conquer
Richard II
Much Ado About Nothing
The Winter's Tale
Macbeth
Everyman
Hamlet
Twelfth Night
Trelawny of the Wells

Producer : ROBERT ATKINS
Costumes for *Trelawny of the Wells* by TOM HESLEWOOD ;
for all other productions by
JOHN GARSIDE. Settings for
Hannele by CHARLES MARFORD ;
for *The Play of the Shepherds*
by HUBERT HINE ; for all
other productions by JOHN
GARSIDE.

1925-6

The Merchant of Venice
Richard III
The Taming of the Shrew
Measure for Measure
Antony and Cleopatra
The Child in Flanders
Harlequin Jack Horner
The Merry Wives of
               Windsor
She Stoops to Conquer
Julius Caesar
As You Like It
The Shoemaker's Holiday

Everyman
Romeo and Juliet
Much Ado About Nothing

Producer : ANDREW LEIGH
Costumes and settings for all
productions by JOHN GARSIDE.

1926-7

King John
A Midsummer Night's Dream
Henry V
The Tempest
Macbeth
The Play of the Shepherds
Christmas Eve
Twelfth Night
Richard III
The Winter's Tale
Othello
Everyman
St Patrick's Day
The Comedy of Errors
Hamlet
The Two Shepherds

Producer : ANDREW LEIGH
Costumes and settings for all
productions by JOHN GARSIDE.

1927-8

The Taming of the Shrew
The Merchant of Venice
Much Ado About Nothing
Henry V
Romeo and Juliet
The Two Noble Kinsmen
The School for Scandal
Everyman
Hamlet
King Lear

Producer : ANDREW LEIGH
Costumes and settings for all
productions by JOHN GARSIDE.
The first four plays in this
season were given at the
Lyric Theatre, Hammer-
smith, while the Old Vic was
closed for re-building.

1928-9

Love's Labour's Lost
The Vikings

As You Like It
Twelfth Night
Adam's Opera
Macbeth
Caste
The Merry Wives of
               Windsor
Mary Magdalene
Henry VIII
The Rivals
Hamlet

Producer : ANDREW LEIGH
Costumes for *Henry VIII* by
CHARLES RICKETTS and PAUL
SMYTH ; settings by PAUL
SMYTH. Costumes and settings
for all other productions by
PAUL SMYTH.

1929-30

Romeo and Juliet
The Merchant of Venice
The Imaginary Invalid
Richard II
A Midsummer Night's Dream
Julius Caesar
As You Like It
The Dark Lady of
               the Sonnets
Androcles and the Lion
Macbeth
Hamlet

Producer : HARCOURT
WILLIAMS
Costumes and settings for all
productions by PAUL SMYTH.

1930-1

Henry IV, Pt I
The Tempest
The Jealous Wife
Richard II
Antony and Cleopatra
Twelfth Night
Arms and the Man
Much Ado About Nothing
King Lear

Producer : HARCOURT
WILLIAMS
Costumes and settings for all
productions by PAUL SMYTH.

1931-2

King John
The Taming of the Shrew
A Midsummer Night's Dream
Henry V
The Knight of the
                Burning Pestle
Julius Caesar
Abraham Lincoln
Othello
Twelfth Night
Hamlet

Producer : HARCOURT
WILLIAMS ; and with JOHN
DRINKWATER for Abraham
Lincoln.

Costumes for The Taming of
the Shrew by FARQUHARSON
SMALL ; for Abraham Lincoln,
Twelfth Night, and Hamlet by
PAUL SMYTH and PETER
TAYLOR-SMITH ; for other
productions by PAUL SMYTH.
Settings for all productions
by PAUL SMYTH.

1932-3

Caesar and Cleopatra
Cymbeline
As You Like It
Macbeth
The Merchant of Venice
She Stoops to Conquer
The Winter's Tale
Mary Stuart
The Admirable Bashville
Romeo and Juliet
The School for Scandal
The Tempest

Producer : HARCOURT
WILLIAMS ; and with JOHN
GIELGUD for The Merchant of
Venice.

Costumes for The Merchant
of Venice by MOTLEY ; for
other productions by PAUL
SMYTH. Settings for Macbeth
by EDWARD CARRICK ; for
The Merchant of Venice by
JOHN GIELGUD ; for other
productions by PAUL SMYTH.

1933-4

Twelfth Night
The Cherry Orchard
Henry VIII
Measure for Measure
The Tempest
The Importance of
                Being Earnest
Macbeth

Producer : TYRONE GUTHRIE

Costumes and settings for
The Cherry Orchard and The
Importance of Being Earnest by
MOLLY McARTHUR ; for
Henry VIII by CHARLES
RICKETTS ; for The Tempest
by JOHN ARMSTRONG. Cos-
tumes for Twelfth Night by
ELIZABETH and MARSH WIL-
LIAMS ; for Measure for Measure
and Macbeth by JOHN ARM-
STRONG. Settings for Twelfth
Night, Measure for Measure,
and Macbeth by WELLS-COATES.

1934-5

Antony and Cleopatra
Richard II
Much Ado About Nothing
St Joan
The Taming of the Shrew
Othello
The Two Shepherds
Hippolytus
Major Barbara
Henry IV, Pt II
Hamlet

Producers : HENRY CASS, all
plays with the exception of
The Two Shepherds, MICHAEL
MacOwan.

Costumes for St Joan by
CHARLES RICKETTS ; settings
by DAVID FFOLKES. Costumes
and settings for Henry IV,
Pt II by FRANCIS BAKER-
SMITH and DAVID FFOLKES ;
for Othello, adapted from E.
McKNIGHT KAUFFER's designs
for Ernest Milton. Costumes
and settings for other productions by DAVID FFOLKES.

1935-6

Peer Gynt
Julius Caesar
The Three Sisters
Macbeth
St Helena
The School for Scandal
Richard III
The Winter's Tale
King Lear

Producers : HENRY CASS, all
plays with the exceptions of
The School for Scandal and
The Winter's Tale, MICHAEL
MacOwan.

Costumes for all productions
by BETTY DYSON. Settings
for Peer Gynt and Richard III
by ERIC NEWTON and BAGNALL
HARRIS ; for other productions
by BAGNALL HARRIS.

1936-7

Love's Labour's Lost
The Country Wife
As You Like It
The Witch of Edmonton
Hamlet
Twelfth Night
Henry V

Producers : TYRONE GUTH-
RIE, all plays with the
exceptions of As You Like
It, ESMÉ CHURCH ; The Witch
of Edmonton, MICHEL SAINT-
DENIS.

Costumes and settings for
Love's Labour's Lost, As You
Like It, and Twelfth Night by
MOLLY McARTHUR ; for The
Witch of Edmonton and Henry
V by MOTLEY ; for The
Country Wife by OLIVER MES-
SEL. Costumes for Hamlet
by OSBORNE ROBINSON, set-
tings by MARTIN BATTERSBY.

1937-8

Pygmalion
Measure for Measure
Richard III
Macbeth

A Midsummer Night's Dream
Othello
The King of Nowhere
Coriolanus

Producers : TYRONE GUTH-
RIE, all plays with the
exceptions of *Macbeth*, MICHEL
SAINT-DENIS ; *The King of
Nowhere*, ESMÉ CHURCH ;
Coriolanus, LEWIS CASSON.

Costumes and settings for
Pygmalion and *The King of
Nowhere* by MOLLY MC-
ARTHUR ; for *Richard III* by
OSBORNE ROBINSON ; for *Mac-
beth* by MOTLEY ; for *A
Midsummer Night's Dream* by
OLIVER MESSEL ; for *Othello*
by ROGER FURSE ; for *Corio-
lanus* by BRUCE WINSTON.
Costumes for *Measure for
Measure* by JOHN ARMSTRONG ;
settings by FRANK SCARLETT.

1938-9

Trelawny of the Wells
Hamlet
Man and Superman
The Rivals
A Midsummer Night's Dream
She Stoops to Conquer
An Enemy of the People
The Taming of the Shrew

Producers : TYRONE GUTH-
RIE, all plays with the
exceptions of *Man and Super-
man*, LEWIS CASSON ; *The
Rivals*, ESMÉ CHURCH ; *She
Stoops to Conquer*, FRANK
NAPIER (with Tyrone Gu-
thrie).

Costumes and settings for
Trelawny of the Wells, *Man
and Superman*, and *An Enemy
of the People* by RUTH KEA-
TING ; for *Hamlet* and *The
Taming of the Shrew* by ROGER
FURSE ; for *The Rivals* by
STEWART CHANEY; for *A
Midsummer Night's Dream* by
OLIVER MESSEL ; for *She
Stoops to Conquer* by DAVID
HOMAN.

1940

King Lear

Producers : LEWIS CASSON
and HARLEY GRANVILLE-
BARKER

Costumes and settings by
ROGER FURSE.

The Tempest

Producers : GEORGE DEVINE
and MARIUS GORING

Costumes and settings by
OLIVER MESSEL.

1941

(At the New Theatre,
London)

King John

Producers : TYRONE GUTHRIE
and LEWIS CASSON

The Cherry Orchard

Producer : TYRONE GUTH-
RIE

Costumes and settings for
King John by FREDERICK
CROOKE ; costumes for *The
Cherry Orchard* by SOPHIA
HARRIS, settings by FRED-
ERICK CROOKE.

1942

(At the New Theatre,
London)

Othello

Producer : JULIUS GELLNER

The Merry Wives of Windsor

Producer : ESMÉ CHURCH

Costumes and settings by
FREDERICK CROOKE.

1943

(At the New Theatre,
London)

The Merchant of Venice

(At the Playhouse,
London)

Abraham Lincoln
The Russians
Blow Your Own Trumpet

Producers : TYRONE GUTH-
RIE (*Abraham Lincoln* and
The Russians) ; ESMÉ CHURCH
(*The Merchant of Venice*) ;
MICHAEL REDGRAVE (*Blow
Your Own Trumpet*).

Costumes and settings for
The Merchant of Venice by
ROGER RAMSDELL ; for
Abraham Lincoln and *The
Russians* by FREDERICK
CROOKE ; for *Blow Your Own
Trumpet* by FELIKS TOPOLSKI.

1944

(At the Lyric Theatre,
Hammersmith)

Guilty

Producer : TYRONE GUTH-
RIE

(At the New Theatre,
London)

Hamlet

Producers : TYRONE GUTH-
RIE and MICHAEL BEN-
THALL

Costumes and settings for
Guilty by REECE PEMBERTON ;
for *Hamlet* by LESLIE HURRY.

1944-5

Peer Gynt
Arms and the Man
Richard III
Uncle Vanya

Producers : JOHN BURRELL,
all plays with the exception
of *Peer Gynt*, TYRONE
GUTHRIE.

Costumes and settings for
Peer Gynt by REECE PEM-
BERTON ; for *Arms and the
Man* by DORIS ZINKEISEN ;
for *Uncle Vanya* by TANYA
MOISEIWITSCH. Costumes for
Richard III by DORIS ZIN-
KEISEN, settings by MORRIS
KESTELMAN.

1945-6

Henry IV, Pt I
Henry IV, Pt II
Oedipus

The Critic
Arms and the Man
Uncle Vanya

Producers : JOHN BURRELL, all plays with the exceptions of *The Critic*, MILES MALLESON ; *Oedipus*, MICHEL SAINT-DENIS.

Costumes and settings for *The Critic* and *Uncle Vanya* by TANYA MOISEIWITSCH ; for *Arms and the Man* by DORIS ZINKEISEN. Costumes for *Henry IV, Pts I and II* by ROGER FURSE, settings by GOWER PARKS. Costumes for *Oedipus* by MARIE-HÉLÈNE DASTÉ, settings by JOHN PIPER.

1946-7

King Lear
An Inspector Calls
Cyrano de Bergerac
The Alchemist
Richard II

Producers : LAURENCE OLIVIER (*King Lear*) ; BASIL DEAN (*An Inspector Calls*) ; TYRONE GUTHRIE (*Cyrano de Bergerac*) ; JOHN BURRELL (*The Alchemist*) ; RALPH RICHARDSON (*Richard II*).

Costumes and settings for *King Lear* by ROGER FURSE ; for *An Inspector Calls* by KATHLEEN ANKERS ; for *Cyrano de Bergerac* by TANYA MOISEIWITSCH ; for *The Alchemist* by MORRIS KESTELMAN ; for *Richard II* by MICHAEL WARRE.

1947-8

The Taming of the Shrew
Richard II
St Joan
The Government Inspector
Coriolanus

Producers : JOHN BURRELL, all plays with the exceptions of *Richard II*, RALPH RICHARDSON ; *Coriolanus*, E. MARTIN BROWNE.

Costumes and settings for *Richard II* by MICHAEL WARRE ; for *The Government Inspector* by FELIKS TOPOLSKI. Costumes for *The Taming of the Shrew* by ALIX STONE and AUDREY CRUDDAS, settings by KATHLEEN ANKERS. Costumes for *St Joan* by ALIX STONE, settings by MICHAEL WARRE. Costumes for *Coriolanus* by KATHLEEN ANKERS, settings by STELLA MARY PEARCE.

1948-9

Twelfth Night
Dr Faustus
The Way of the World
The Cherry Orchard
The School for Scandal
Richard III
The Proposal
Antigone

Producers : JOHN BURRELL (*Dr Faustus*, *The Way of the World* and *Richard III*) ; ALEC GUINNESS (*Twelfth Night*) ; HUGH HUNT (*The Cherry Orchard*) ; LAURENCE OLIVIER (*The School for Scandal*, *The Proposal*, and *Antigone*).

Costumes and settings for *Twelfth Night* by MICHAEL WARRE ; for *Dr Faustus* by MORRIS KESTELMAN ; for *The Way of the World* by BERKELEY SUTCLIFFE ; for *The Cherry Orchard* by TANYA MOISEIWITSCH ; for *The School for Scandal* by CECIL BEATON. Costumes for *Richard III* by DORIS ZINKEISEN, settings by MORRIS KESTELMAN. Costumes for *The Proposal* and *Antigone* by SOPHIA HARRIS, settings by ROGER RAMSDELL, décor by ROGER FURSE.

Appendix B

PLAYERS at the Old Vic theatre, 1914–40 ; with Old Vic companies at the New, Playhouse, and Lyric theatres, London, between 1941 and 1944, and with the Old Vic Theatre Company at the New Theatre, 1944–9.

A

Abbott, John	1936–7
Abney, W.	1938–9
Adams, Bruce	1936–7
Adams, Eileen	1922–3
Adams, Miriam	1932–3
Adams, Phyllis	1924–5
Addyman, Elizabeth	1924–7
Adeney, Eric	1927–30
,, ,,	1937–8
Ainley, Richard	1929–32
Ainsworth, John	1945–6
Alden, John	1937–8
Aldridge, Claudia	1935–6
Allam, Betty	1938–9
Allan, Elizabeth	1927–8
Allardyce, Grace	1926–8
Allen, Edward	1923–4
Allen, Eileen	1914–15
Allen, Evelyn	1931–2
,, ,,	1933–4
Allen, Frederick	1935–6
Allen, John	1932–4
Allen, May	1937–9
Ambrose, W.	1938–9
Anderson, James	1915–16
Anderson, Jessie	1924–5
Anderson, Judith	1937–8
Anderson, Robin	1931–2
Anderton, Jean	1917–19
Andre, Elene	1926–7
Andrews, Harry	1938–9
,, ,,	1946–9
Angel, Heather	1926–7
Angelo, Irma	1932–3
Anthony, Susan	1929–30
Appleyard, Margaret	1933–4
Archard, Bernard	1938–9
Archdale, Alec	1929–30
Armstrong, William	1919–20
Arnold, John	1946–7
Arundel, Frank	1932–3
Arundel, Jean	1937–8
Arundell, Dennis	1933–4
Ashby, Clement	1938–9

Ashby, Clement	1941–4
Ashcroft, Peggy	1932–3
Asherson, Renée	1940
,, ,,	1941–4
,, ,,	1947–8
Ashton, Elizabeth	1921–3
Ashwin, Michael	1934–5
Atkins, Alfred	1940
Atkins, Robert	1915–16
,, ,,	1920–1
,, ,,	1922–5
Atkinson, Rosalind	1941–4
,, ,,	1946–8
Austin, Sylvia	1929–30
Aylmer, Felix	1934–5
Ayrton, Norman	1948–9

B

Babbage, Wilfred	1928–9
Backus, Molly	1934–5
Bacon, Jane	1920–4
Baddeley, Angela	1915–16
,, ,,	1937–8
Bailey, Caroline	1933–5
Bailey, Gordon	1914–15
Bailey, John	1935–6
Baird, Dorothy	1941–4
Baker, Dorothy	1920–1
Baker, Frank	1941–4
Baker, Iris	1928–9
Baker, L. Kingsley	1922–5
Ball, Phyllida	1935–6
Bamford, Freda	1926–7
Bannerman, Kay	1941–4
Barker, G.	1936–7
Barker, Molly	1926–7
Barlow, Hester	1936–7
Barlow, Ronald	1948–9
Barnes, Kenneth	1926–7
Barnett, Orlando	1916–19
Barr, Patrick	1936–7

Barran, George	1918–19
Barrett, Charles	1941–4
Barrington, Doreen	1930–1
Barry, Philip	1917–18
Barton, Mary	1920–1
Barton, Reyner	1921–4
,, ,,	1927–9
Baskcombe, Laurence	1933–4
,, ,,	1936–7
Bateman, Leah	1916–17
Bateson, Timothy	1948–9
Baxter, David	1938–9
Baxter, Jane	1948–9
Baxter, Lindsay	1933–4
Baylis, Ethel	1916–17
Baynton, Henry	1917–18
Bazeley, G.	1923–4
Beaumont, Robert	1941–4
,, ,,	1948–9
Beck, Helen	1948–9
Beck, Roger	1936–7
Beckley, Gladys	1915–16
Beckwith, Martin	1941–4
Beedell, Christopher	1947–8
Beers, H. Stanley	1928–30
,, ,, ,,	1931–2
Beeston, G.	1923–4
Beldon, Eileen	1918–19
,, ,,	1948–9
Bell, Clapham	1930–1
Belmore, Guy	1936–7
Bench, Mary	1938–9
Bennett, Elsie	1914–15
Bennett, Frederick	1936–9
,, ,,	1941–4
Bennett, Leonard	1926–7
Bennett, Vivienne	1934–6
,, ,,	1937–8
Benson, George	1938–9
Bent, Buena	1934–5
Benthall, Michael	1938–9
Bentley, Wilfred	1925–6
Berendt, Rachel	1928–9
Beresford, Helen	1919–20
Beresford, Isabel	1915–16

Fildes, Phyllis	1920–1	Garside, John	1921–3	Green, Nigel	1948–9
Filmer, A. E.	1915–16	,, ,,	1924–8	Green, William	1922 3
Firth, Ivan	1917–18	,, ,,	1941–4	Greenidge, Terence	1934–5
,, ,,	1919–20	Garvin, Ursula	1924–5	Greenwood, Edwin	1915–16
Firth, Kenneth	1941–4	Gauntlett, Vera	1937–8	Greenwood, Miles	1938–9
Fitzgerald, John	1941–4	Gavin, Anthony	1948–9	Greet, Ben	1914–18
Fitzsimon, Simon	1941–4	Gaye, Freda	1941–4	,, ,,	1928–9
Flanigan, Joan	1936–7	Genn, Leo	1934–7	Greet, Clare	1915–16
Fletcher, Campbell	1918–20	Ghazzawi, El	1938–9	Gregory, Dora	1937–8
Fletcher, Eileen	1933–4	Gibson, James	1941–4	Greig, Margaret	1932–3
Folkard, Janet	1935–7	Gibson, Reginald	1931–2	Grenville, Margot	1920–1
Folliott, Bernadette	1936–7	Gielgud, John	1929–31	Griffiths, Lucy	1941–4
Foote, Adela	1914–15	,, ,,	1940	Grimley, Bertram	1933–4
,, ,,	1916–17	Giles, Ethel	1944–5	Grimley, Fink	1933–4
Foote, Gladys	1914–15	Gill, Basil	1933–4	Groser, Antony	1941–4
,, ,,	1916–17	Gill, David	1919–21	Grosset, Jean	1934–5
Foote, Mildred	1915–18	Gilroy, Francis	1937–8	Guinness, Alec	1936–7
Foote, Veronica	1915–18	Gingold, Hermione	1914	,, ,,	1938–9
Forbes, Brenda	1927–8	Glasby, Althea	1921–3	,, ,,	1940
Forbes, Meriel	1938–9	Glass, John	1937–8	,, ,,	1946–8
Forbes-Robertson,		Glaze, William	1941–4		
Jean	1927–8	Glendinning, Ethel	1930–2		
Forbes-Robertson,		Glennie, Robert	1922–4		
Peter	1941–4	Glenville, Peter	1938–9	**H**	
Fordred, Dorice	1923–5	Godfrey, Royden	1945–6		
,, ,,	1935–6	Godley, G. N.	1923–4	Habunek, Vlado	1936–7
Forwyth, Robert	1925–6	Golden, Michael	1941–4	Hacon, Marie	1937–8
Foss, Alan	1933–6	Goodchild, Zillah	1936–7	Hagan, George	1933–4
Foss, G. R.	1917–19	Goodhart, Frances	1934–5	,, ,,	1941–4
Fothergill, Philip	1927–33	Goodliffe, Michael	1937–8	Haggard, Stephen	1940
Fox, Bert	1941–4	Goodwin, Ernest	1915–16	Hall, Elizabeth	1929–30
Fox, F. C.	1929–30	Goolden, Richard	1933–4	Hall, Evelyn	1934–5
Fox, Lee	1941–4	,, ,,	1936–7	Hall, Ronald	1937–8
Fox, William	1932–3	Gordon, Donald	1937–8	Hall, William	1915–16
France, Alexis	1930–1	Gordon, Ellen	1929–30	Halstan, Margaret	1914–15
,, ,,	1937–8	Gordon, Kenneth	1937–8	Hambling, Arthur	1941–4
Francelli, Mario	1937–8	Gordon, Ruth	1936–7	Hamilton, Keith	1919–20
Francis, J.	1923–4	Goring, Marius	1931–5	Hamilton, Mary	1920–2
Francis, Mollie	1922–5	,, ,,	1936–7	,, ,,	1923–4
,, ,,	1929–30	,, ,,	1940	Hankamer, Mariane	1938–9
Frank, Edmund	1923–4	Goring-Thomas, Vera	1928–9	Hannen, Hermione	1938–9
Franklyn, John	1935–6	Gough, Michael	1936–7	,, ,,	1941–4
Fraser, Ralph	1941–4	Gowans, Wendy	1929–30	Hannen, Nicholas	1940
French, Elsie	1934–5	Graham, Morland	1932–6	,, ,,	1941–4
French, Leslie	1929–33	Grahame, Ailsa	1936–8	,, ,,	1944–7
Friston, Stella	1920–1	,, ,,	1941–4	Hannen, Peter	1931–2
Frith, Arthur	1920–1	Grahame, Margot	1941–4	Hanray, Lawrence	1941–4
Frith, John Leslie	1914–15	Grain, A. Corney	1914–16	Harald, Frank	1937–8
Furmedge, Edith	1918–19	Grange, John	1941–4	Harben, Joan	1930–1
Furse, Judith	1931–3	Grantham, Wilfred	1930–1	Harcourt, James	1941–4
Furse, Roger	1932–3	Granville, Ursula	1935–6	Hardingham,	
		Graves, Diana	1936–7	Andrew	1919–20
		,, ,,	1941–4	Hardwicke,	
		Gray, Alfred	1941–4	Sir Cedric	1914–15
G		,, ,,	1944–5	,, ,, ,,	1948–9
		Gray, Lois	1929–30	Hardy, Betty	1944–5
Gabain, Marjorie	1917–18	,, ,,	1931–2	Hardy, Geoffrey	1936–8
Gabriel, Gladys	1924–5	Gray, Willoughby	1938–9	Hare, Ernest	1933–5
Gamage, Dorothy de	1937–8	Green, Charles	1921–2	,, ,,	1936–7
Garland, Gwendolyn	1914–15	Green, Dorothy	1930–1	,, ,,	1938–9
Garley, John	1945–9	,, ,,	1934–5	,, ,,	1941–4

Harker, Frederick	1920–1
,, ,,	1925–6
Harker, Nancy	1921–3
Harper, Ethel	1914–16
,, ,,	1920–1
,, ,,	1922–5
Harris, Clare	1932–3
Harris, Crafton	1932–3
Harris, L.	1936–7
Harris, Gabrielle	1915–16
Harris, Percy	1928–9
Harris, Richard	1923–4
Harris, Robert	1931–2
,, ,,	1940
Harris, Topsy	1924–5
Hart-Davis, Rupert	1927–8
Harvey, Joy	1933–4
Harvey, Rupert	1918–19
,, ,,	1920–4
,, ,,	927–8
Harvey-Kelly, Hugh	1938–9
Haslewood, Guy	1935–6
Hassall, Christopher	1933–4
Hatch, Phyllis	1933–5
Hawkins, Jack	1940
Hawkins, Stockwell	1918–20
Hawley, Doris	1920–1
Hawtrey, Anthony	1930–1
Hawtrey, Charles	1938–9
Haye, Helen	1935–6
Hayes, George	1923–5
,, ,,	1936–7
Haynes, Audrie	1919–21
,, ,,	1928–9
Haynes, Dora	1919–20
Haynes, Margaret	1921–3
Haythorne, Edmund	1919–21
Heard, Daphne	1936–7
Hearne, Reginald	1946–9
Heathcote, Humphrey	1944–5
Heathcote, Thomas	1938–9
,, ,,	1948–9
Heavey, Jack	1937–8
Helmy, Hassan	1938–9
Helpmann, Robert	1937–9
,, ,,	1941–4
Henderson, Donald	1933–4
Henning, Basil	1914–15
Henri, Gerald	1936–7
Henry-May, Pamela	1929–31
Herbert, Jean	1919–20
Herbert, Katherine	1918–19
Herd, John	1933–4
Hermansen, Ruth	1934–5
Heron, Gilbert	1918–19
Hershey, Alta	1933–4
Hewitt, Francis	1936–8
Hickman, Charles	1932–3
,, ,,	1941–4
Hicks, Ogna	1918–20

Higginson, Margaret	1937–8
Hildebrandt, Stanley	1938–9
Hilditch, Kathleen	1938–9
,, ,,	1941–4
Hill, Crooms	1916–17
Hillyard, Alfred	1926–8
Hilton, Constance	1917–19
Hine, Hubert	1920–4
Hinton, Anthony	1947–8
Hitchman, Michael	1944–5
Hobling, Lorna	1935–6
Hodson, Gerald	1947–8
Hoey, Iris	1936–7
Hole, Dora	1924–5
Holland, Christopher	1917–18
Holland, Elspeth	1931–2
Holliday, Geoffrey	1938–9
Holloway, Baliol	1925–7
Holloway, Edwin	1914–15
Holme, Stanford	1941–4
Holme, Timothy	1946–7
Home, Cecil	1926–8
Homfray, Phyllis	1930–1
Hope, Cyprian	1926–7
Hope, Vida	1944–5
Horne, David	1934–5
Horne, Denise	1937–8
Hornsby, Nancy	1934–6
Horrey, Frederic	1941–4
Hossack, J. Laird	1922–3
Houston, Hugh	1936–8
Howard, Anthony	1938–9
Howard, Trevor	1947–8
Howe, George	1930–1
Howe, Harry	1937–8
Howell, Peter	1944–5
Hoyle, James	1936–9
Hudd, Ruby	1914–15
Hudd, Walter	1941–4
Hudson, Gilbert	1920–1
Hull, Mary	1928–9
Hulme, Anthony	1938–9
Hunt, Martita	1929–30
,, ,,	1931–2
,, ,,	1937–8
Hunter, Oliver	1948–9
Hunter, Peggy	1928–9
Huntley, Raymond	1935–6
Hutchison, Douglas	1921–2
Hyde, Audrey	1920–1
Hyde, Millicent	1919–21
Hyson, Dorothy	1938–9

I

Igel, Leonide	1934–5
Ilma, Dorothy	1914–16
Ingram, George	1937–8
Ingram, Jeanne	1938–9
Irish, Jun., Frank	1937–8

Irving, Ellis	1937–8
Isham, Sir Gyles	1929–30
,, ,, ,,	1937–8
Israel, G.	1936–7
Ittner, Alice	1934–5
Ives, Franklyn	1927–8

J

Jack, Janet	1936–8
Jack, Stephen	1924–5
Jackson, Freda	1936–7
,, ,,	1938–9
,, ,,	1941–4
Jackson, Ray	1945–6
Jacobs, Sadie	1938–9
James, Douglas	1919–20
James, Francis	1929–30
James, Joseph	1945–6
James, Ronald	1933–4
Jameson, John	1935–7
Jameson, Pauline	1947–9
Jarman, Betty	1938–9
Jarman, Peggy	1938–9
Jarman, Reginald	1916–21
Jeans, Ursula	1933–4
,, ,,	1936–7
,, ,,	1938–9
Jefferies, Douglas	1931–2
Jefferson, Ross	1929–30
Jenkyns, Sydney	1936–7
Jennings, Sandra	1946–7
Jerome, Gerald	1937–8
Jessel, Genevieve	1937–8
John, Evan	1933–4
John, Frances	1938–9
Johns, Glynis	1935–6
Johnson, Celia	1947–8
Johnson, Raymond	1933–5
Johnstone, Viola	1944–5
Johnstone, Violet	1931–2
Jones, Edith Lester	1921–2
Jones, John	1937–8
Jones, Kathleen	1929–30
Jones, Mary	1941–4
Jones, Merry	1937–8
Jones, Owen	1936–7
Jones, Ralph	1947–8
Jordan, Patrick	1946–8
Joss, Iris Fraser	1914–15
Joye, Janet	1946–7
Judson, Alan	1937–8

K

Kahn, Florence	1935–6
Kane, Wyman	1932–3
Kann, Lily	1941–4

Maddox, Diana	1944–6	Milford, George	1941–4	Nesbitt, Cathleen	1934–5
Madison, Margaret	1938–9	Millard, Lionel	1926–7	,, ,,	1940
Magor, Prudence	1930–1	Miller, Dorothy	1945–6	Neville, John	1947–8
Maitland, Marne	1940	Miller, Gordon	1937–8	Nevinson, Nancy	1944–5
Maitland, Ruth	1934–5	Mills, John	1938–9	New, E.	1936–7
Malandrinos, André	1941–4	Milton, Ernest	1918–22	Newbold, Brenda	1936–9
Malcolm, Roy	1941–4	,, ,,	1924–5	Newbold, Jill	1934–6
Malleson, Miles	1945–6	,, ,,	1926–8	Newcomb, Mary	1934–5
Malone, Dinah	1941–4	,, ,.	1941–4	Newlands, Roy	1924–7
Maloney, Pat	1931–2	Mitchell, Julien	1946–7	,, ,,	1936–7
Malvery, Christian	1930–1	Mitchell, Mabel	1928–9	Newton, Robert	1936–7
Mango, Alec	1936–8	Mitchell, Nancye	1944–5	Ney, Marie	1924–5
,, ,,	1941–4	Mollison, Ian	1933–4	,, ,,	1935–6
Mapp, Neville	1936–7	Monk, William	1925–7	,, ,,	1937–8
,, ,,	1938–9	,, ,,	1945–6	Nichol, John	1946–7
Marchant, Herbert	1936–8	Moody, John	1933–4	Nicholas, Maurice	1944–5
Marfleet, Grace	1922–3	,, ,,	1937–8	Nicholls, Anthony	1938–9
Marford, Charles	1924–8	Moore, H.	1929–30	Nichols, Ernest	1924–5
Marlé, Arnold	1941–4	Moore, Terence	1934–5	Nicholson, Nora	1914–15
Marriott, Arliss	1935–6	Moore, William	1914–16	,, ,,	1938–9
Marsden, Robert	1941–4	Morell, André	1938–9	Nicholson, Richard	1924–5
Marshall, Fred	1946–7	,, ,,	1940	Nicholson, Ronald	1922–5
Marshall, Peter	1945–6	Morena, Frederic	1914–15	Nilsom, H.	1931–2
Marsh-Dunn,		Morgan, Charles	1933–4	Nobel, Phillida	1936–7
Bertram	1926–7	Morgan, Diana	1934–5	Nolte, Pietro	1946–8
Martin, M.		Morgan, Kenneth	1938–9	Nono, Cecilia	1922–3
Macdonald	1914–15	Morgan, Terence	1948–9	,, ,,	1924–5
Martindale, Ursula	1930–1	Morgan, Thomas	1936–7	,, ,,	1928–9
Martineau, Guy	1921–4	Morley, Robert	1937–8	Norman, Maurice	1937–8
Martlew, Mary	1948–9	Morris, Ian	1938–9	,, ,,	1946–7
Mason, James	1933–4	Morris, Rose	1944–5	Norman,	
Massingham, Dorothy	1926–7	Morriston, Brenda	1935–6	Norman V.	1916–18
Matthews, Douglas	1935–7	Morrogh, James	1931–2	Norris, Mary	1932–3
Matthews, Olive	1938–9	Mortimer, H.	1917–18	Nowell, Amy	1925–6
Mattinson, Douglas	1922–4	Morton, Jessica	1941–4	Nuttall, George	1937–8
Maturin, Elizabeth	1938–9	Moubrey, Lilian	1915–19		
Maugham, Mona	1915–16	Mowbray, Phyllis	1930–1		
Maxwell, Meg	1948–9	Mucklow, June	1937–8		
Mayer, Ferdinand	1938–9	Mulvey, Phyllis	1920–1		
,, ,,	1941–4	,, ,,	1924–5	**O**	
Mayer, G. A.	1923–4	Mummery, Phyllis	1923–4		
,, ,, ,,	1926–8	Munday, Penelope	1947–9	Oakleigh, Joanna	1916–18
Maynard, Siegfried	1938–9	Murch, Margaret	1914–15	Oakley, Edith	1924–5
Maynard, Trevor	1933–4	Murray, Ethel	1941–4	Oates, Cecily	1925–6
Meads, Ernest	1915–23	Murray, Stephen	1936–8	O'Brien, Terence	1916–17
,, ,,	1925–6	Myer, Joan	1920–1	,, ,,	1937–8
Measor, Beryl	1934–5			O'Callaghan, E.	1926–7
Mellor, Philip	1947–9			O'Connor, Cavan	1925–6
Mercer, Charles	1937–8			O'Dowd, Joseph	1914–15
Mercer, Thomas	1937–8			O'Dwyer, Katherine	1921–2
Meredith, Yolande	1938–9	**N**		O'Leary, Ursula	1947–8
Merefield, Bernard	1948–9			Olgar, Chris	1914–15
Merivale, Jack	1937–8	Nano, Michael	1933–4	Olivier, Sir Laurence	1936–8
Merlin, Monica	1927–8	Napier, Alan	1934–5	,, ,, ,,	1944–7
Merritt, George	1934–5	Napier, Ella	1917–18	,, ,, ,,	1948–9
Metcalfe, Queenie	1915–17	Napier, Frank	1931–5	Omar, Margaret	1914–15
Michael, Ralph	1931–2	,, ,,	1937–9	Orkin, Andre	1944–5
Midgley, Gladys	1922–3	Napper, John	1914–16	Ormonde, Doris	1918–19
,, ,,	1924–5	Neale, Noreen	1926–7	Osman, Elizabeth	1945–6
Miles, Bernard	1941–4	Neilson, Evelyn	1922–5	Ottoway, James	1937–8
,, ,,	1947–8	Nelson, Gwendolen	1926–8	,, ,,	1941–4
		Nelson, John	1929–30		

Oughton, Winifred	1916–20
„ „	1927–8
„ „	1938–9
Outhwaite, Walter	1944–7
Owen, Elizabeth	1924–5
Owen, Mardale	1931–2

P

Pack, Charles	1927–8
Packenham, Simona	1935–6
Page, Joy	1924–5
Palmer, Betty	1937–9
Palmer, Elsa	1930–1
Palmer, Irene	1934–5
Palmer, Penelope	1934–5
Pantin, Nell	1929–30
Parker, Althea	1937–9
Parker, Beve	1937–8
Parker, Brian	1945–7
Parkin, Rex	1932–3
Parks, Murray	1929–30
Parry, Richard	1937–8
Parsons, David	1934–5
Passmore, Dorothy	1919–20
Paterson, E. H.	1919–20
Patrick, Rosalind	1929–30
Patrick, Sara	1926–7
Payne, Laurence	1938–9
„ „	1941–4
Payton, H.	1914–15
Pearson, Mary	1925–6
Peduzzi, Victor	1929–31
Peel, Eileen	1936–7
Pellowe, Patricia	1931–2
Penley, Derrick	1948–9
Penna, Tarva	1914–15
Pepler, Margaret	1938–9
Perceval, Robert	1947–8
Percival, Dolly	1917–18
Percival, Robert	1915–17
Percy, Esmé	1938–9
„ „	1941–4
Perkins, Arthur	1941–4
Perridge, John	1921–2
Perrin, Michael	1936–8
Perry, Helen	1934–5
Peters, Joseph	1917–19
Peters, Myrtle	1924–5
Petersen, Frances	1921–2
Petley, Frank	1941–4
Petrie, Hay	1919–24
„ „	1927–8
Phelps, Anthony	1937–8
Phelps, Bridget	1934–6
Phillips, Alice	1914–15
Phillips, Arthur	1914–15
Phillips, Eric	1928–31
Phipps, Nicholas	1931–2

Pickard, Helena	1927–8
Pickard, Peggy	1927–8
Pidgeon, Audrey	1941–4
Pilbeam, Arnold	1927–8
Pillitz, Doris	1927–8
Piper, Fred	1921–2
Pittar, B. A.	1914–15
„ „ „	1916–17
Pohl, Hortense te Water	1931–2
Pohlmann, Erich	1946–7
Pole, Collwyn	1924–6
Pole, Katherine	1924–5
Poliakoff, Vera	1937–8
Porter, Neil	1924–7
„ „	1929–30
„ „	1937–8
Portman, Eric	1926–8
„ „	1930–1
Potter, Betty	1917–20
„ „	1935–7
Potter, Frank	1915–16
Powell, Margaret	1932–3
Powell, May	1923–4
„ „	1925–6
Prentice, Derek	1933–4
Price, Dennis	1941–4
Price, Nancy	1914–15
Price, Nettie	1946–7
Pritchard, Joan	1926–7
Priwin, Marion	1935–7
Pugh, James	1936–7
„ „	1941–4
Purdy, Doreen	1929–31

Q

Quartermaine, Leon	1933–4
Quayle, Anthony	1932–3
„ „	1935–6
„ „	1937–9
Quitak, Oscar	1945–7
Quixley, Kitty	1922–3

R

Radley, Beatrice	1919–20
Rae, John	1936–8
Raghan, Michael	1944–8
Ralph, David	1941–4
Ramsden, Nancy	1934–5
Randall, Zoe	1934–5
Raphael, Oliver	1929–30
Ratcliffe, Thomas	1935–6
Rawson, Tristan	1937–8
„ „	1941–4
Raymond, Cyril	1914–15
Redgrave, Michael	1936–7

Redington, Michael	1948–9
Redman, Joyce	1944–7
Reed, Maxwell	1945–6
Reed, Owen	1938–9
Reis, June	1944–5
Relph, George	1944–7
„ „	1948–9
Rentoul, Patience	1927–8
Reynolds, Martyn	1917–18
Rice, E.	1929–30
Richards, Aubrey	1946–8
Richards, Ivy	1928–9
Richards, Winifred	1918–19
Richardson, F. J.	1914–15
Richardson, Gordon	1929–31
Richardson, Gwendoline	1918–19
Richardson, Jean	1920–1
Richardson, Myrtle	1935–6
Richardson, Sir Ralph	1930–2
„ „ „	1937–8
„ „ „	1944–7
Richman, Edith	1936–7
Richmond, Maureen	1933–4
Richmond, Valentine	1933–4
„ „	1938–9
Ricks, Claude	1923–6
Riddle, Richard	1929–32
Rignold, Marie	1938–9
Riley, Mollie	1935–6
Ripley, Dorothy	1914–15
Ritchie, Richard	1931–2
Ritchie, Ronald	1934–5
Robere, Eve	1936–7
Roberts, Deri Vaughan	1941–4
Roberts, Ewan	1946–7
Roberts, Iris	1918–28
Roberts, Mabel	1928–9
Robertshaw, Jerrold	1914–15
Robertson, Constance	1914–15
Robertson, Stuart	1921–2
Robins, Joy	1931–2
Robinson, Gilbert	1944–7
Robinson, Maureen	1933–4
Robson, Flora	1933–4
„ „	1941–4
Robson, Nellie	1920–2
Robson, Renee	1918–19
Rogers, Joan	1915–16
Rose, George	1944–8
Rose, Ian	1937–8
Rosmer, Milton	1936–7
Ross, Donald	1941–4
Ross, Eric	1916–19
Ross, Mignonne	1926–7
Ross, Oriel	1940
Ross, Patrick	1933–5
Ross-Shore, Mary	1914–15

INDEX

Names of plays (and of books, periodicals and the like) are printed in italic. No entries appear either under *Old Vic* or *Shakespeare* for reasons which the title of this book makes apparent ; but references to general subjects (see, for example, *Press criticism*) which apply only to the activities of the Old Vic are so described throughout the index.